A LONGMAN
LATIN READER

CATULLUS AND HORACE

Selections from Their Lyric Poetry

Prepared by Andrew C. Aronson and Robert Boughner

LONGMAN

Catullus and Horace: Selections From Their Lyric Poetry

Longman Inc., 95 Church Street, White Plains, N. Y. 10601

Associated companies:
Longman Group Ltd., London
Longman Cheshire Pty., Melbourne
Longman Paul Pty., Auckland
Copp Clark Pitman, Toronto
Pitman Publishing Inc., New York

Authors: **Andrew C. Aronson**, Sidwell Friends School, Washington, D.C.
Robert Boughner, Mary Washington College, Fredericksburg, Virginia
Series Editor: **Professor Gilbert Lawall**, University of Massachusetts,
Amherst
Consultants: **Jane Harriman Hall**, Mary Washington College,
Fredericksburg, Virginia
Richard A. LaFleur, University of Georgia,
Athens, Georgia
Robert E. Morse, Saint Andrew's School,
Boca Raton, Florida

Executive editor: Lyn McLean
Production editor: Elsa van Bergen
Text and cover designer: Gayle Jaeger
Production supervisor: Judith Stern

ISBN 0-582-36750-6

Compositor: r/tsi typographic company, inc.
Printer: R. R. Donnelley & Sons Company

88 89 90 91 92 9 8 7 6 5 4 3 2 1

CONTENTS

Introduction   1

POEMS OF CATULLUS (*with first line*)   7

(*5*) Vīvāmus, mea Lesbia, atque amēmus   9

(*8*) Miser Catulle, dēsinās ineptīre   11

(*12*) Marrūcīne Asinī, manū sinistrā   13

(*13*) Cēnābis bene, mī Fabulle, apud mē   15

(*22*) Suffēnus iste, Vāre, quem probē nōstī   17

(*43*) Salvē, nec minimō puella nāsō   19

(*46*) Iam vēr ēgelidōs refert tepōrēs   21

(*49*) Disertissime Rōmulī nepōtum   23

(*51*) Ille mī pār esse deō vidētur   25

(*53*) Rīsī nescio quem modo ē corōnā   27

(*70*) Nūllī sē dīcit mulier mea nūbere mālle   27

(*72*) Dīcēbās quondam sōlum tē nōsse Catullum   29

(*73*) Dēsine dē quōquam quicquam bene velle merērī   31

(*75*) Hūc est mēns dēducta tuā, mea Lesbia, culpā   31

(*76*) Sīqua recordantī benefacta priōra voluptās   33

(*83*) Lesbia mī praesente virō mala plūrima dīcit   35

(*84*) Chommoda dīcēbat, sī quandō commoda vellet   37

(*85*) Ōdī et amō. Quārē id faciam, fortasse requīris?   39

(*86*) Quīntia fōrmōsa est multīs. Mihi candida, longa   41

(*87*) Nūlla potest mulier tantum sē dīcere amātam   43

(*92*) Lesbia mī dīcit semper male nec tacet umquam   43

(*96*) Sī quicquam mūtīs grātum acceptumve sepulcrīs   45

(*101*) Multās per gentēs et multa per aequora vectus   47

(*109*) Iūcundum, mea vīta, mihi prōpōnis amōrem   48

POEMS OF HORACE (*with first line*)   49

(*I.3*) Sīc tē dīva potēns Cyprī   51

(*I.5*) Quis multā gracilis tē puer in rosā   55

(*I.9*) Vidēs ut altā stet nive candidum 57

(*I.11*) Tū nē quaesieris, scīre nefās, quem mihi, quem tibi 61

(*I.14*) Ō nāvis, referent in mare tē novī 63

(*I.22*) Integer vītae scelerisque pūrus 65

(*I.23*) Vītās īnuleō mē similis, Chloē 67

(*I.37*) Nunc est bibendum, nunc pede līberō 69

(*I.38*) Persicōs ōdī, puer, apparātūs 73

(*II.3*) Aequam mementō rēbus in arduīs 75

(*II.14*) Ēheu fugācēs, Postume, Postume 77

(*III.13*) Ō fōns Bandusiae, splendidior vitrō 81

(*III.30*) Exēgī monumentum aere perennius 83

(*IV.7*) Diffūgēre nivēs, redeunt iam grāmina campīs 85

Vocabulary 86

Credits 92

ACKNOWLEDGMENTS

A reader of this sort would have been impossible without the help and advice of our students at Mary Washington College and the Sidwell Friends School. We dedicate this book to teachers, colleagues, friends, parents, and grandparents who have supported us through the years.

INTRODUCTION

Catullus and Horace, the two poets you are about to read, occupy a privileged place in the history of Western literature. They are Rome's greatest lyric poets, and they are important links in the chain that connects the earlier Greek lyric poets to the long literary tradition extending from Rome to our own day. The poetry they wrote, lyric, was named after the lyre, a musical instrument to which the words of the poems were originally sung. Of the early Greek lyric poets, two names are important to us here, Sappho and Alcaeus. They were both from the island of Lesbos near modern-day Turkey, and they were contemporaries of each other in the seventh century B.C. Lyric poetry, being a deeply personal art form, expressed for them feelings and thoughts about things closest to the heart—love, sorrow, desire, political freedom, the shortness of human life, and death; their lyric verses departed dramatically from the standard epic and heroic themes of a Homer or Hesiod. At the other end of the Greek literary spectrum stands Callimachus, resident poet in the third century B.C. of the famous library of Alexandria in Egypt, who in emphasizing style and technical brilliance bequeathed to the Roman poets a poetry that was refined and chiseled, full of obscure allusions and unexpected references, and often playful and noncommittal. Such were the two streams of influence for Catullus and Horace: from Sappho and Alcaeus a precedent for frank, sometimes coarse, disclosure of feelings, desires, and reflections, and from Callimachus an insistence on the artistry and technique behind the expression and a certain aloofness and distance between the poet and the audience.

CATULLUS

Of Catullus, we know very little. Tradition says that his full name was Gaius Valerius Catullus and that he was born about 84 B.C. in the northern city of Verona. He belonged to an upper-middle-class family that could afford to own villas at Sirmio and Tivoli and host Caesar during one of his northern trips.

Catullus moved to Rome, as many youths did, to seek fame and fortune. There he joined a loosely related group of poets and thinkers who were given the Greek name *neoteroi* (the "newer ones") and the Latin title **novī poētae**. The names of some of Catullus' comrades have come down to us in his poetry: Calvus, Cinna, and Caecilius. The poetic creed of these poets drew on the principles set forth by the Hellenistic poets of Alexandria and especially by Callimachus, mentioned above, who called a big book a "great evil" and practiced a poetry of refinement, pithiness, erudition, and detachment.

In Rome, Catullus had an intense love affair with a woman whom he has immortalized in his poetry under the pseudonym of Lesbia. Two poems of his—the only two written in the sapphic meter—seem to frame the affair. Poem 51 is a translation of a poem of Sappho's, and it reveals strong desire and fascination for a certain woman. The second, poem 11, which is not included in this reader, is a bitter dismissal of a woman, probably the same Lesbia. Other poems explore the early infatuation and secret meetings, the growing doubt about Lesbia's fidelity, and the painful disillusionment at the end.

In using the name Lesbia for the woman of his heart, Catullus accomplished three things: he paid tribute to the love poet Sappho, who was from the island of Lesbos; he firmly established himself in the tradition of love lyric, which reached back to Sappho; and he has tantalized us with a three-syllable name metrically interchangeable with a notorious contemporary of his, Clodia. Sister of Clodius Pulcher, a famous gang leader and enemy of Cicero, Clodia attracted much attention because of the social circles in which she traveled and the rumors of her numerous affairs during and after her marriage to the patrician and consul Metellus, who died mysteriously in 59 B.C. Cicero has given us a full, if biased, description of her in his *Pro Caelio*, in which he defends Caelius against charges brought by Clodia. There are too many facts—the chronology, the rumors about her affairs, the similarity in form between the names Lesbia and Clodia—not to risk making positive identification, but risk it is because we do not have any testimony earlier than that of the second-century A.D. writer Apuleius, who states that the Lesbia of Catullus' poetry was Clodia.

In 57 B.C. Catullus spent a year in Bithynia, a Roman province in Asia Minor, where with high hopes and ambitions for financial reward and excitement he had followed the appointed governor, Memmius. A year later, unhappy and with no personal gain, Catullus bade farewell to the East and returned home to Italy where, not long after, possibly in 54 B.C., he died of unknown causes.

Catullus wrote with great feeling and personal intensity. His short poems on the affair with Lesbia cover a wide range of emotions, and his other poems also vary in tone and content, as, for example, a light, playful tribute to his yacht, a sad memorial to his dead brother, invective and coarse ridicule heaped upon friends and enemies, and long poems on marriage. Throughout all the poems selected for this volume are features that are typical of Catullus. The poems are direct and to the point, and we know immediately to whom the poem is addressed (sometimes it is to Catullus himself). Certain words quickly characterize what is right or wrong about a person or a poem. **Venustus** ("charming"), **facētiae** ("wit"), and **urbānus** ("sophisticated") are positive words that reflect the tenets of the **novī poētae**. **Invenustus** ("uncharming"), **īnfacētus** ("witless"), and **rūs** ("countryside") define the opposite. We discover, in addition, that the poet presents himself in a variety of guises or **persōnae** (**persōna** is Latin for "mask") throughout his poems, endorsing spontaneity at one moment, serious commitment at another, and given sometimes to emotional outbursts and personal involvement, at other times to detachment and self-analysis.

One hundred and sixteen poems have come down to us, of which three, poems 18–20, were probably not written by Catullus. Traditionally, the collection has been divided into three groups: poems 1–60 in various meters; 61–64, which are longer and more ambitious; and 65–116, all in elegiac couplets. Whether or not this is the order in which Catullus first published his poems, we do not know; they lack an obvious chronological or thematic progression, but subtle developments and connections between the poems do suggest intentional numbering by the poet.

HORACE

The life of Quintus Horatius Flaccus is better documented and better known to us. Horace was born on 8 December 65 B.C., in Venusia, a town located far southeast of Rome on the Via Appia. The region of his birth and upbringing, Apulia, was not especially prosperous: most of the inhabitants subsisted on grazing and herding. His father, a freedman, took Horace to Rome for a first-class education in the capital.

Later, Horace pursued his studies in Athens, where many Roman intellectuals and ambitious students went. Surrounded by politically outspoken members of the anti-Caesar, antidictatorial Republican party, Horace was swept up in the movement and joined Brutus and Cassius, who had fled to Greece following the assassination of Caesar. Greece was once again an arena where Romans settled their disputes by warfare, and at the battle of Philippi in 42 B.C. Octavian soundly defeated Brutus and Cassius and quashed all dreams of a revival of the Republic. Horace returned to Rome without position and without property. First, he earned a job for himself as a recordkeeper for the quaestors, the magistrates responsible for the financial activities of the government. Horace's fortune improved dramatically in 39 B.C., when Vergil, then working on his first major work, the *Eclogues*, introduced him to Maecenas, a patron of poets and Augustus' most trusted adviser after Agrippa. Maecenas was impressed by Horace's literary promise; he invited him to join his coterie of poets and later gave him the "Sabine Farm," a place to compose poetry and a symbol in his poetry of simplicity and contentment. From then until his death in 8 B.C., Horace devoted himself to his *Epodes*, *Satires*, *Odes*, *Letters*, and *Art of Poetry.*

The first three books of *Odes* were published as a unit in 23 B.C.; the fourth book was published ten years later. In the *Odes* Horace set himself the task of bringing the poetic forms and themes of the Greek lyric poets Sappho, Alcaeus, and Pindar to Latin poetry. He did more, however, than just imitate them; he created wonderfully fluid and subtle verses unlike anything else in Latin. The technique is highly artistic: word order and placement are stretched and used for maximum impact, imagery and allusion are extensive and colorful, and the meter is demanding and intricate. Some of the intimacy between poet and audience, which we feel with Catullus, however, is lost. The poems of Horace are more philosophical, meditative, and elusive, and the situations of the poems seem more contrived.

HORACE'S EPICUREANISM

Two prominent philosophies of Horace's day were Stoicism and Epicureanism. Stoicism was named after the *Stoa Poikile*, or "Painted Porch," from which Zeno (335–263 B.C.), the sect's founder, preached. He stressed civic and political commitment and an inner discipline that helped free one from the fluctuations and uncertainties of daily life. The other school, Epicureanism, was descended from Zeno's contemporary, Epicurus (341–270 B.C.). It placed more emphasis on the pursuit of moderate, not excessive, pleasure through satisfaction of basic needs and avoidance of pain. The difference between the two is to some extent symbolized by the fact that Zeno taught in a public place in the Athenian agora, or marketplace, while Epicurus retreated to his famous garden to spend time talking and living among a close circle of friends.

A brief description of the Epicureanism that we find in Horace's work may help to put his poems in context. According to this philosophy, we are creatures of the day who at death dissolve into nothingness. The gods exist, but they enjoy an existence outside the human realm and do not interfere with human events. Thus the Mars, Neptune, and Venus we meet in Horace are poetic symbols and allusions to a literary mythology, not real gods. We, as humans, have some control over the immediate circumstances of life, but there is an unknown design—called variously Necessity, Fortune, or Jupiter—that shapes our lives, causes sudden shifts in our fortune, and obscures the future beyond this day. Therefore, says Horace, we must not worry about what the future life or afterlife has in store for us. Instead, we should enjoy this moment—summed up pithily in the expression he coined, **Carpe diem** ("Seize the day")—and free ourselves from the greed, political ambitions, and superstitious fears that interfere with this precious enjoyment of life. A glass of wine in the company of friends, surrounded by a simple estate, describes clearly the Horatian ideal.

METER

It is not commonly known or appreciated that the habit of reading silently to oneself appeared late in Western history, somewhere in the third or fourth centuries of this era, and that literature, and in particular, poetry, was composed with a listening not a reading audience in mind. Among the ancients, the meter or beat of a poem was the mold into which the lines fit in order for the poem to be considered whole and complete, performing much the same service as a frame for a painting or a melody for the words of a song. Without meter, a poem would have been indistinct and without identity. The choice of a meter had much to do with the poet's intention; one meter may have been chosen for its long, stately lines, one for a light, humorous beat, and another for its association with earlier epic or love poets. In return, each meter put specific demands on the poet regarding the choice of words (some words may fit easily into one meter and not into another) and the word order. Special attention should therefore be given to the meter of each poem as you read it.

ON TRANSLATING

Two caveats before you begin translating. One is that you avoid a mere translation of single words. Often a poet will sacrifice the logic or clarity you might expect of a prose author in order to open up levels of meaning and depths of feeling through the use of unexpected associations, allusions to mythology or distant lands, unusual word order, and poetic devices such as repetition, parallelism, and exaggeration. As you translate, be concerned with both the literal meaning of the words and the image, emotion, or train of thought of the poet.

The other temptation, that of being more interested in making some immediate sense of the poem than in basing your translation on an accurate knowledge of the vocabulary and grammar, also should be avoided. All meaning must be rooted in proper translation of the Latin, so if you read by instinct, slow down and pay close attention to, among other things, endings, proper agreement of nouns and adjectives, and the correct identification of verb forms.

4

POETIC DEVICES

The following is a list of the poetic devices that are identified in the notes and questions accompanying the poems of Catullus and Horace. The terms are italicized and defined at their first occurrence, which is noted in the following list. You will find many other examples of these devices in the poems; the definitions in the list below will help you identify them.

Allegory: Horace I.14, question 2. A work in which the action and characters are understood both literally and as referring in a one-to-one correspondence to something else, usually historical, moral, or philosophical in nature.

Alliteration: Catullus 5, question 3. The repetition of initial consonant sounds in two or more closely situated words.

Anaphora: Catullus 5, question 3. Repetition of a word at the beginning of successive phrases or clauses.

Assonance: Catullus 5, question 3. The close recurrence of similar vowel sounds.

Asyndeton: Catullus 22, question 8. The absence of conjunctions.

Caesura: Catullus 8, metrical heading. Word-end within a metrical foot, frequently coinciding with a pause in the sense of the line.

Chiasmus: Catullus 84, question 1. An arrangement of pairs of words in opposite order within a line or between lines: for example, the cat jumped in, out jumped the mouse.

Connotation: Catullus 84, question 3. Positive or negative associations that a word may have.

Consonance: Catullus 46, question 2. The close recurrence of similar consonant sounds.

Diaeresis: Catullus 70, metrical heading. Word-end between metrical feet, frequently coinciding with a pause in the sense of the line.

Diction: Catullus 76, question 4. The choice and arrangement of words to fit the subject matter.

Diminutive: Catullus 8, note to line 18. Words with suffixes, such as **-ellus, -olus,** and **-ullus,** that denote smallness and that are often used to express affection, delicacy, humor, or mockery.

Dramatic irony: Catullus 70, question 1. A situation in which the audience knows something that the literary character does not.

Hendiadys: Catullus 12, note to line 2. The use of two nouns joined by a conjunction in place of an expected noun and adjective: for example, "in joke and wine" for "in tipsy jest."

Hyperbole: Catullus 5, question 3. The use of exaggeration.

Imagery: Catullus 73, question 3. The use of descriptive language to represent people or objects, often appealing to our senses.

Inceptive verbs: Catullus 46, note to line 3. Verbs that denote through a suffix, such as **-scō,** the beginning of an action.

Interlocked word order: Catullus 87, question 1. An arrangement of two pairs of words so that one word of each pair is between the words of the other in an *abab* pattern.

Irony: Catullus 49, question 1. A device by which a speaker or writer expresses one meaning but expects the audience to be aware of another, usually opposite, meaning.

Line framing: Catullus 13, note to line 2. The framing of a line of poetry by two words that are grammatically related, such as a noun and its modifier or a verb and its subject.

Litotes: Catullus 43, question 2. A figure of speech in which a statement is made through the negation of its opposite, such as, "That was *no small* accomplishment."

Metaphor: Catullus 8, question 4. An implied comparison between things without the words *like* or *as*.

Metonymy: Horace I.22, note to line 20. The use of a word that evokes something else through close association without actually naming it.

Oxymoron: Catullus 46, note to line 1. A contradictory statement, such as "chilly warm days."

Parody: Catullus 13, question 5. An imitation of a conventional literary form or theme in a lighthearted or ridiculing manner.

Persona: Catullus 8, question 2. The projection of one or several aspects of a writer's personality onto a literary character.

Polysyndeton: Catullus 22, question 8. The use of more conjunctions than necessary.

Propempticon (Greek *propemptikon*): Horace I.3, question 1. A traditional "send-off" poem that generally includes grief and protest over the departure of a friend, prayers for a safe voyage and return, and a curse on the inventor of sailing.

Repetition: Catullus 22, question 7. The use of the same word or phrase two or more times in a poem to emphasize a point or feeling.

Rhetorical irony: Catullus 70, question 1. A situation in which the speaker says one thing but means another.

Simile: Catullus 76, question 6. A comparison between two things, expressed by the words *like* or *as*.

Synecdoche: Horace I.14, note to line 7. The figure of speech in which a part represents the whole.

Tmesis: Horace I.9, note to line 14. The separation of a compound word into its parts with other words placed in between.

Tone: Catullus 43, question 4. The poet's attitude toward the subject matter.

Transferred epithet: Catullus 51, note to line 11. An adjective used to describe one noun instead of another that it would normally modify.

POEMS OF CATULLUS

Poēta Rōmānus

METER: hendecasyllabic (Greek for "eleven syllables"), one of the most common of the meters used by Catullus. The pattern of the line is:

$$\underline{\smile}\,\underline{\smile}\,-\,\smile\,\smile\,-\,\smile\,-\,\smile\,-\,\underline{\smile}$$
$$\underset{\smile\;\underline{\smile}}{}$$

1 **Vīvāmus**: how do you translate the three hortatory subjunctives **vīvāmus, amēmus** (1), and **aestimēmus** (3)? *Lesbia, -ae (f), the woman to whom the poem is addressed (see p. 2 in the Introduction).

2 **rūmor, rūmōris** (m), rumor, gossip, story. **senum**: what declension, case, and number? **sevērus, -a, -um,** severe in judgment, stern, strict. The comparative may be translated literally or with "rather" or "quite."

3 **omnēs**: often in poetry an adjective is separated by several words or even a line from the noun it modifies. Which word does **omnēs** modify?

    aestimō (1), to estimate, consider, rate, value.

    as, assis (m), bronze Roman coin (the smallest unit of Roman currency, similar to a penny). The value of an item goes into the genitive in Latin: **ūnius assis,** "at only an **as**," "as worth just a penny." Note the short i in the pronunciation of **ūnius** here.

4 *occidō, occidere (3), occidī, occāsum, to fall, set.

5 **nōbīs**: translate as either a dative of reference, "for us," or as dative of agent with **dormienda** (6), "by us." **semel**, once.

6 *perpetuus, -a, -um, everlasting, continuous, uninterrupted.
    est . . . dormienda: what form is **dormienda**? What construction is this?

7 *mī: = mihi. *bāsium, -ī (n), kiss.

8 *dein: = deinde.

9 **usque**, continuously, immediately, right on to.

10 **fēcerīmus**: future perfect indicative. An indicative may be used in a **cum** clause to express simply time when (compare the use of **cum** with the subjunctive in circumstantial clauses). Note the long i in the pronunciation of the word here.

11 **conturbō** (1), to throw into confusion, scramble, stir up.
    nē sciāmus: what construction is this?

12 *quis, quid, anybody, somebody, anything, something. This indefinite pronoun is commonly found after **sī, nē, nisi,** and **num**. **nē quis malus**: "so that somebody evil may not. . . ." **invideō, invidēre (2), invīdī, invīsum,** to cast an evil eye, look maliciously at, be envious, be jealous. **possit**: what mood and tense?

13 **tantum**: accusative, "so great a number."
    sciat: what construction do you expect after a verb like **sciō**?

CATULLUS 5

Give Me a Thousand Kisses!

The first three lines of this poem introduce the themes of living, loving, and valuing. How are each of these themes developed in the rest of the poem?

> Vīvāmus, mea Lesbia, atque amēmus,
> rūmōrēsque senum sevēriōrum
> omnēs ūnius aestimēmus assis!
> Sōlēs occidere et redīre possunt;
> 5 nōbīs cum semel occidit brevis lūx,
> nox est perpetua ūna dormienda.
> Dā mī bāsia mīlle, deinde centum,
> dein mīlle altera, dein secunda centum,
> deinde usque altera mīlle, deinde centum.
> 10 Dein, cum mīlia multa fēcerīmus,
> conturbābimus illa, nē sciāmus,
> aut nē quis malus invidēre possit,
> cum tantum sciat esse bāsiōrum.

1. In particular, what is Catullus referring to in lines 2 and 3? What are the *r* and *s* sounds meant to imitate?

2. In lines 4–6, what common observation is Catullus making? What are the possible meanings of *lūx* and *nox* in terms of human existence? Why is *sōlēs* plural and *lūx* singular?

3. Why would conclusions drawn from lines 4–6 lead to the series of demands in lines 7–9? Find examples of *alliteration* (repetition of initial consonant sounds in two or more closely situated words), *assonance* (close recurrence of similar vowel sounds), *anaphora* (repetition of a word at the beginning of successive phrases or clauses), and *hyperbole* (exaggeration) in lines 7–9.

4. What two explicit reasons does Catullus give in lines 11–13 for mixing up the number of kisses he and Lesbia have had? Explain how either development could have endangered the outpouring of kisses.

5. The verb *conturbāre* (11) may allude to shaking up an abacus board. What role do numbers play in this poem?

6. Read this poem aloud and in meter. What is the effect of the two elisions in line 1? Which letters should you accentuate in lines 7–10? What happens in lines 8–9 as the numbers pile up?

7. How well does this adaptation by Ben Jonson (1572–1637) succeed?

> Come, my Celia, let us prove
> While we may the sports of love;
> Time will not be ours forever,
> He at length our good will sever.
> Spend not then his gifts in vain;
> Suns that set may rise again,
> But if once we lose this light,
> 'Tis with us perpetual night.
> Why should we defer our joys?
>
> Fame and rumor are but toys.
> Cannot we delude the eyes
> Of a few poor household spies?
> Or his easier ears beguile,
> So removed by our wile?
> 'Tis no sin love's fruit to steal;
> But the sweet theft to reveal,
> To be taken, to be seen,
> These have crimes accounted been.

METER: choliambic (a variant of the iambic line, devised by Greek poets for satire and mockery; the term means "limping iambic." The limping effect has been achieved by making the next to the last syllable long instead of short). The pattern is:

$$\overset{\smile}{-}-\,|\,\smile-\,|\,\overset{\smile}{-}-\,|\,\smile-\,|\,\smile-\,|\,-\overset{\smile}{}$$

A *caesura* (word-end within a metrical foot, frequently coinciding with a pause in the sense of the line) often falls in the middle of the third foot.

1 **Catulle**: vocative, from **Catullus, -ī** (*m*).
  *dēsinō, dēsinere (3), **dēsiī, dēsitum** (+ *infinitive*), to give up, stop. Translate the hortatory subjunctives **dēsinās** (1) and **dūcās** (2) as imperatives.
  ineptiō, ineptīre (4), to play the fool, be a fool.
2 **quod . . . dūcās**: supply **id** as the understood antecedent of **quod**. Word order: **dūcās (id), quod perīsse vidēs, perditum (esse)**. **perīsse**: from the verb **pereō, perīre**. **perīsse**: = **periisse**. What tense is the infinitive? ***perdō, perdere** (3), **perdidī, perditum**, to destroy, ruin, lose. **perditum esse**: what tense and voice?
  dūcō, dūcere (3), **dūxī, ductum**, (here) to consider, (in line 4) lead.
3 ***fulgeō, fulgēre** (2), **fulsī**, to shine, glitter. **Fulsēre**: = **Fulsērunt**.
  *quondam, once. ***candidus, -a, -um**, bright, dazzling.
4 **ventitō** (1), to come often.
5 **nōbīs**: = **ā mē**. **nūlla**: supply **puella**.
6 **ibi**, then, at that time. **illa multa**: with **iocōsa** after **cum**. **iocōsa, -ōrum** (*n pl*), playful things, playful moments.
9 ***iam . . . nōn**, no longer. **illa**: i.e., **puella**. **volt**: = **vult**. **impotēns, impotentis**, lacking self-control, headstrong, powerless, weak in will. Which definition fits the context best? **nōlī**: what form is this?
10 **quae**: supply **eam** as antecedent of **quae** and object of **sectāre**. **sector, sectārī** (1), **sectātus sum**, to chase after. **sectāre**: the present singular imperative of the deponent verb **sector**. The imperative of deponent verbs ends in **-re** in the singular and **-minī** in the plural.
11 **obstinātus, -a, -um**, resolved, determined. **perferō, perferre** (*irreg.*), **pertulī, perlātum**, to bear through, endure. ***obdūrō** (1), to be firm, persist.
13 **requīrō, requīrere** (3), **requīsīvī, requīsītum**, to look for again, seek after.
  *invītus, -a, -um, unwilling. **invītam**: **tē** is understood.
14 **nūlla**: adverbial, "not," "not at all" (a colloquial usage).
15 **scelestus, -a, -um**, wicked, unfortunate, wretched. **vae tē**, woe to you.
  quae: take this interrogative adjective with **vīta**.
16 **adeō, adīre** (*irreg.*), **adiī, aditum**, to approach, visit. ***bellus, -a, -um**, pretty, nice, cute.
17 **Cuius esse dīcēris**: first translate this literally, then find a more idiomatic way of saying it. In the 3rd conjugation, an *e* is used for both the present and future of the 2nd person singular passive. How does the length of the vowel help you decide the tense?
18 **bāsiō** (1), to kiss. **Cui**: dative of reference; here, translate as a genitive, "Whose . . .?" **labellum, -ī** (*n*), little lip. Catullus is fond of using *diminutives* (words with suffixes, such as **-ellus, -olus**, and **-ullus**, that denote smallness) to express a variety of feelings such as affection, delicacy, humor, or mockery.
  mordeō, mordēre (2), **momordī, morsum**, to bite, nibble.
19 **dēstinātus, -a, -um**, fixed, decided, firm, steadfast.

CATULLUS 8

Catullus, Stop Being a Fool!

Catullus, hopelessly in love, exhorts himself to pull out of the love affair.
Memories of happy moments and of the girl, however, weaken his resolve.

Miser Catulle, dēsinās ineptīre,
et quod vidēs perīsse perditum dūcās.
Fulsēre quondam candidī tibī sōlēs,
cum ventitābās quō puella dūcēbat
5   amāta nōbīs quantum amābitur nūlla;
ibi illa multa cum iocōsa fiēbant,
quae tū volēbās nec puella nōlēbat,
fulsēre vērē candidī tibī sōlēs.
Nunc iam illa nōn volt: tū quoque impotēns nōlī,
10   nec quae fugit sectāre, nec miser vīve,
sed obstinātā mente perfer, obdūrā.
Valē, puella. Iam Catullus obdūrat,
nec tē requīret nec rogābit invītam.
At tū dolēbis, cum rogāberis nūlla.
15   Scelesta, vae tē, quae tibī manet vīta?
Quis nunc tē adībit? Cui vidēberis bella?
Quem nunc amābis? Cuius esse dīcēris?
Quem bāsiābis? Cui labella mordēbis?
At tū, Catulle, dēstinātus obdūrā.

1. **Divide the poem into different sections according to the use of key transitional words (e.g., *quondam*). What is the mood of each section and what causes the shifts in mood? What role does time play in these sections?**
2. **It is commonly accepted that poets project different aspects of themselves onto the real or imaginary characters of their poems. A poet may, for instance, adopt the identity of a wise traveler, homeless youth, or loving parent. This adopted identity is called *persōna* (Latin for "mask"). What *persōna* does Catullus assume for himself in this poem? Why does he address himself in the 3rd person?**
3. **Explain what Catullus means in line 2.**
4. **Lines 3 and 8 act as a frame for the memory of an earlier time. How can you interpret the words *candidī . . . sōlēs* metaphorically (*metaphor* is an implied comparison between two objects)? What difference does the substitution of *vērē* (8) for *quondam* (3) make in the meaning of the repeated line?**
5. **This poem presents a classic confrontation between the will and the emotions (sparked by memories of happier days). Which side seems stronger? What weakens the poet's resolve to end the affair? Support your answer by reference to the poem.**
6. **Reread the poem and note words or phrases that are repeated. What is significant about the repeated words? Why would repetition be such a major part of this poem? Find examples of words with a double *l*. What pattern do they form?**
7. **Why are limping iambics an appropriate meter for this poem?**

METER: hendecasyllabic (see Catullus 5).

1 **Marrūcīnus Asinius**: an acquaintance of Catullus. The order of the **nōmen** (**Asinius**) and **cognōmen** (**Marrūcīnus**) may be reversed, as it is here. **manū sinistrā**: why are these two words in the ablative?

2 **ūteris**: present or future? What is the clue?
in iocō atque vīnō: translate literally as, "in joke and wine," or as an example of *hendiadys* (the use of two nouns joined by a conjunction in place of an expected noun and adjective), "in tipsy jest."

3 ***linteum, -ī** (*n*), napkin. The Romans brought their own napkins to parties.
neglegēns, neglegentis, negligent, careless. What degree, case, and number is the adjective? What noun do you need to supply?

4 **salsus, -a, -um**, salty, humorous, witty. **Fugit tē**: "It escapes you," "That's where you are wrong." **ineptus, -a, -um**, silly, foolish.

5 **quamvīs**, ever so, highly, extremely. **sordidus, -a, -um**, sordid, filthy, disgraceful. **invenustus, -a, -um**, uncharming, unattractive.

6 **mihi? . . . Polliōnī**: in what case are these two words and why?
Polliō, Polliōnis (*m*), brother of Asinius and most likely the Roman orator and historian Gaius Asinius Pollio (76 B.C.–A.D. 4).

7 **fūrtum, -ī** (*n*), theft. **vel talentō**: "for even a talent of gold" (a talent was a large amount of gold or silver).

8 **mūtō** (1), to change, exchange, undo. **mūtārī**: what form, tense, and voice? **velit**: from what verb? Identify the mood, tense, and construction.
lepos, lepōris (*m*), charm.

9 **differtus, -a, -um** (+ *gen.*), stuffed with, full of. **facētiae, -ārum** (*f pl*), wit.

10 ***quārē**, for which reason, therefore. **hendecasyllabī, -ōrum** (*m pl*) (*Greek loan word*), hendecasyllables, eleven-syllable verses (the meter of this poem and one often used by Catullus for satire and abuse as well as for love poems, such as poem 5). **trecentī, -ae, -a**, three hundred.

12 **quod**: relative pronoun and subject of **movet**. Identify the antecedent, gender, and number.
aestimātiō, aestimātiōnis (*f*), price.

13 ***vērum**, but, but rather. **mnēmosynum, -ī** (*n*) (*Greek loan word*), souvenir, memento. **sodālis, sodālis** (*m*), companion, friend.

14 **sūdārium, -ī** (*n*), sweat cloth, handkerchief, napkin. **Saetabus, -a, -um**, Saetaban, from Saetabis (a town in Spain known for its linen goods). **Hibērī, Hibērōrum** (*m pl*), Spaniards, (here) Spain (consult the map on p. 20 for important place names used in this text).

15 **mihi mūnerī**: double dative, "to me for (the purpose of) a gift," "to me as a gift."
Fabullus: he and **Vērānius** (16) were friends of Catullus.

16 **haec**: i.e., the **sūdāria** (14). **amem**: supply **ut** (which is often left out after impersonal verbs like **necesse est**) and translate lines 16–17 in this order: **necesse est (ut) haec amem ut** (as) **Vērāniolum meum et Fabullum** (amō).

17 **Vērāniolum**: what does the diminutive express here? (See note on line 18 of poem 8.) How can you best translate it into English?

CATULLUS 12

A Thief at Large

What has Asinius Marrucinus stolen? How does Catullus threaten to get it back? Why is it valuable?

Marrūcīne Asinī, manū sinistrā
nōn bellē ūteris: in iocō atque vīnō
tollis lintea neglegentiōrum.
Hoc salsum esse putās? Fugit tē, inepte:
5 quamvīs sordida rēs et invenusta est.
Nōn crēdis mihi? Crēde Polliōnī
frātrī, quī tua fūrta vel talentō
mūtārī velit—est enim lepōrum
differtus puer ac facētiārum.
10 Quārē aut hendecasyllabōs trecentōs
exspectā, aut mihi linteum remitte,
quod mē nōn movet aestimātiōne,
vērum est mnēmosynum meī sodālis.
Nam sūdāria Saetaba ex Hibērīs
15 mīsērunt mihi mūnerī Fabullus
et Vērānius; haec amem necesse est
ut Vērāniolum meum et Fabullum.

1. **What words characterize Asinius and his crime in lines 1–5? What is Catullus emphasizing about the nature and style of the crime and about the attitude of the thief?**
2. **Why does Catullus mention Pollio, Asinius' brother (6–9)?**
3. **What threat does Catullus make in lines 10–11? What rhetorical device does he use to highlight the threat? Do you take him seriously?**
4. **The poem ends on a sentimental note. Why does Catullus really want the napkin back? Is Catullus one of the *neglegentiōrēs* in line 3? If so, who is really the guilty person in this poem and of what is he guilty?**
5. **In line 1, look closely at the two pairs of words. How do they echo each other? Where else in this poem does Catullus play with the sounds of words?**

METER: hendecasyllabic (see Catullus 5).

1 *cēnō (1), to dine.   mī: vocative singular of **meus**, often used with close friends. **Fabullus**, -ī (m), a dear friend of Catullus (see Catullus 12).   **apud** (+ acc.), at the home of, with.

2 **paucīs . . . diēbus**: how do you translate the ablative of time here? Note how Catullus has framed the line with these two words. Find another example of *line framing* in this poem.   *dī: = **deī** (nom. pl.).   **faveō, favēre** (2), **fāvī, fautum** (+ dat.), to favor.   **sī . . . favent**: equivalent to our expression, "God willing."

3 *afferō, affere (irreg.), attulī, allātum, to bring. The future perfect **attuleris** is used in the first half (protasis) of a future more vivid conditional sentence. Where is the second half or conclusion (apodosis)? What is the tense of the verb in the apodosis?

4 *candidus, -a, -um, white, fair-skinned, striking.

5 *sal, salis (m), salt, humor, wit.   **cachinnus**, -ī (m), loud laughter.   **omnibus cachinnīs**: "all kinds of loud laughter."

6 *venustus, -a, -um, charming, attractive, handsome. In what case is the adjective here? What noun is understood?   **noster**: Catullus often uses the plural possessive adjective instead of the singular; translate, "my."

7 **tuī Catullī**: genitive of possession with **sacculus** (8).

8 **plēnus**, -a, -um (+ gen.), full of.   **sacculus**, -ī (m) (diminutive), small sack, bag, purse, pouch.   **arānea**, -ae (f), spider web, cobweb.

9 **contrā** (adv.), in return.   **merus**, -a, -um, undiluted, pure.   *amor, amōris (m), love, (plural) affection.

10 **seu . . . est**: "or if there is anything sweeter or more elegant," "or (you will receive) what is more agreeable or more refined."

11 **unguentum**, -ī (n), perfume.   **quod**: what are the antecedent, gender, number, and case of this relative pronoun and of the one in line 13?   **meae puellae**: how do you decide which one of three possible cases this is?

12 *dōnō (1), to present, give as a gift.   **dōnārunt**: = **dōnāvērunt**.   **Venerēs Cupīdinēsque**: "(all) Venuses and Cupids."

13 **olfaciō, olfacere** (3), **olfēcī, olfactum**, to smell.

14 **ut tē faciant**: on what word does this clause depend? What is the name of this construction?   *nāsus, -ī (m), nose.

. . . unguentum dabo. . . .

14

CATULLUS 13

An Unusual Dinner Invitation

What offer does Catullus make in the first two lines of the following poem and how is it undercut by what follows?

Cēnābis bene, mī Fabulle, apud mē
paucīs, sī tibi dī favent, diēbus,
sī tēcum attuleris bonam atque magnam
cēnam, nōn sine candidā puellā
5   et vīnō et sale et omnibus cachinnīs.
Haec sī, inquam, attuleris, venuste noster,
cēnābis bene; nam tuī Catullī
plēnus sacculus est arānēārum.
Sed contrā accipiēs merōs amōrēs,
10   seu quid suāvius ēlegantiusve est:
nam unguentum dabo, quod meae puellae
dōnārunt Venerēs Cupīdinēsque;
quod tū cum olfaciēs, deōs rogābis
tōtum ut tē faciant, Fabulle, nāsum.

1. What does Catullus want Fabullus to bring to the dinner party? Why would these things be important for this dinner? By the end of the poem, how are we to understand the words *cēnābis bene*?
2. In lines 7–8, what reason does Catullus give for his unexpected request? Do you believe him? Why would he say this?
3. What does Catullus promise to give Fabullus in return? What makes it so special?
4. What is the humor in the last two lines?
5. Discuss the ways in which this poem is a *parody* (an imitation of a conventional literary form or theme in a lighthearted or ridiculing manner) of a proper invitation.
6. Thomas McAfee, a modern poet, has created a dialogue across centuries in the following poem. From the poems you have read, which *persōnae* of Catullus does McAfee appear to admire and envy? What is meant in the last line?

If I had your gall, Catullus,
I wouldn't worry about the phone
  bill
Or the end of the month
Or how much you owe for last
  year's
Income tax. You could live
On ink and my sweat. I saw
The dinner invitation you sent:
*Bring your own food (and make
  sure
I'll like it), a beautiful woman,*

*And a good wine. Don't forget
Witty talk, and you have to do
The laughing.*
              I know. You don't
Have to tell me. He might even show
And you could get drunk and flirt
With the woman. If he doesn't,
You'd be depressed anyway.

METER: choliambic (see Catullus 8).

1 **Suffēnus, -ī** (*m*), the poet about whom Catullus is writing this poem. None of his works has survived. **Vārus, -ī** (*m*), the person to whom this poem is addressed. **probē,** thoroughly, well. **nōstī:** = **nōvistī.**

2 **dicāx, dicācis,** witty. ***urbānus, -a, -um,** urbane, sophisticated.

3 **īdem:** what noun do you need to supply? **longē plūrimōs:** "very, very many."

4 **esse:** take with **perscrīpta** in line 5 to form a perfect passive infinitive. Why is the infinitive used here? **illī:** dative of agent. **mīlia . . . plūra:** supply "things" or "verses" in your translation. **aut . . . aut,** "or . . . or even." **decem:** supply **mīlia.**

5 **perscrībō, perscrībere** (3), **perscrīpsī, perscrīptum,** to write at length. **sīc ut fit:** "as is common." **palimpsestum, -ī** (*n*) (*Greek loan word*), palimpsest (writing material that has been used several times, mentioned here as an example of cheap or secondhand parchment. Its root meaning is "scraped again.")

6 **referō, referre** (*irreg.*), **rettulī, relātum,** to record, jot down. **relāta:** supply **sunt.** Following the word **relāta** is a list of expensive procedures that Suffenus has used to bind his poetry. Before you translate the list, you may want to smooth the transition by inserting in your translation words, such as, "on the contrary, there are. . . ." **carta, -ae** (*f*), paper, papyrus. **rēgius, -a, -um,** royal, high-quality, expensive. **liber, librī** (*m*), book, roll.

7 **umbilīcus, -ī** (*m*), navel, knob (used in rolling papyrus). **lōrum, -ī** (*n*), strap, leather tie. **ruber, rubra, rubrum,** red. **membrāna, -ae** (*f*), thin skin, scroll cover.

8 **dērigō, dērigere** (3), **dērēxī, dērēctum,** to guide, line (a page). **plumbum, -ī** (*n*), lead (used for making lines on paper). **pūmex, pūmicis** (*m*), pumice stone (used for polishing and smoothing). **omnia:** subject of **dērēcta . . . et . . . aequāta. aequō** (1), to make level, smooth.

9 **bellus, -a, -um,** handsome, dashing.

10 **ūnus, -a, -um,** merely, only. Take with **caprimulgus. caprimulgus, -ī** (*m*), goat-milker, goatherd. **fossor, fossōris** (*m*), ditchdigger.

11 **rūrsus,** on the contrary, on the other hand. **vidētur:** supply **esse. tantum** (*adv.*), so much, so. **abhorreō, abhorrēre** (2), **abhorruī,** to differ, to be different. I.e., from his earlier self.

12 **quid putēmus:** a deliberative subjunctive, "what are we to think?" **Quī:** the antecedent is **īdem** in line 14; for a smoother translation, try, "the same man (**īdem**), who . . . , is. . . ." **scurra, -ae** (*m*), a wit, clever man.

13 **aut . . . scītius:** "or if something is sharper than this," "or even a bit sharper than that." **scītus, -a, -um,** knowing, shrewd, sharp.

14 ***īnfacētus, -a, -um,** witless, dull-witted, crude. **rūs, rūris** (*n*), countryside, farmlands.

15 ***simul:** = **simul ac,** as soon as. ***poēma, poēmatis** (*n*) (*Greek loan word*), poem. **attingō, attingere** (3), **attigī, attāctum,** to touch, undertake, put one's hand to.

16 **aequē . . . ac . . . cum,** equally . . . as when. ***beātus, -a, -um,** happy.

17 ***gaudeō, gaudēre** (2), **gāvīsus sum,** to rejoice, find delight, take pleasure.

18 **nīmīrum,** clearly. **idem omnēs fallimur:** "we are all deceived the same way," "we all make the same mistake." Note that **idem,** with a short *i*, is neuter. **fallō, fallere** (3), **fefellī, falsum,** to mislead, (passive) be deceived, be mistaken.

19 **in aliquā rē:** "in some situation or other." The second foot of this line consists of three short syllables. **Suffēnum:** "as a Suffenus," "to be like Suffenus."

20 **possīs:** what mood is this and why? **Suus . . . error:** "One's own defect," "One's imperfection." **cuique:** what case and number? What are the nominative singular forms of this indefinite pronoun? **attribuō, attribuere** (3), **attribuī, attribūtum,** to allot, assign.

21 **mantica, -ae** (*f*) wallet, knapsack. A substantive (noun or pronoun) must be understood with the partitive genitive; translate **manticae quod** as "any of the knapsack that. . . ."

CATULLUS 22

On a Local Poetaster

Suffenus is a charming person, but as a poet—. Still, there is a little bit of Suffenus in us all.

Suffēnus iste, Vāre, quem probē nōstī,
homō est venustus et dicāx et urbānus,
īdemque longē plūrimōs facit versūs.
Putō esse ego illī mīlia aut decem aut plūra
5 perscrīpta, nec sīc ut fit in palimpsestō
relāta: cartae rēgiae, novī librī,
novī umbilīcī, lōra rubra, membrānae,
dērēcta plumbō et pūmice omnia aequāta.
Haec cum legās tū, bellus ille et urbānus
10 Suffēnus ūnus caprimulgus aut fossor
rūrsus vidētur: tantum abhorret ac mūtat.
Hoc quid putēmus esse? Quī modo scurra
aut sī quid hāc rē scītius vidēbātur,
īdem īnfacētō est īnfacētior rūre,
15 simul poēmata attigit, neque īdem umquam
aequē est beātus ac poēma cum scrībit:
tam gaudet in sē tamque sē ipse mīrātur.
Nīmīrum idem omnēs fallimur, neque est quisquam
quem nōn in aliquā rē vidēre Suffēnum
20 possīs. Suus cuique attribūtus est error;
sed nōn vidēmus manticae quod in tergō est.

1. In lines 1–8, why does Catullus specifically approve of Suffenus the person and not Suffenus the poet? Cite Latin words to support your answer.
2. Compare lines 6–8 of this poem to the opening lines of poem 1, where Catullus asks to whom he should dedicate his work:

   Cui dōnō lepidum (*charming*) novum libellum
   āridā (*dry*) modo pūmice expolītum (*polished*)?

   Although both passages place an emphasis on appearances, what is the essential difference between Catullus' *libellus* and Suffenus' *librī*? How, according to Catullus, might the outer binding reflect the inner content differently for the two poets?
3. According to lines 9–14, what transformation is noticed when one reads Suffenus' poetry?
4. Why would Suffenus' behavior in lines 15–17 be so annoying to Catullus?
5. What observation on human nature does Catullus make in lines 18–21?
6. How many elisions can you find in line 4? What do the elisions add to the meaning of this line?
7. *Repetition* is an effective device in poetry; the same word or phrase used two or three times can emphasize a point or feeling. Which words are repeated in this poem and why?
8. *Polysyndeton* is the use of more conjunctions than necessary, and *asyndeton* is the absence of conjunctions. Find an example of the latter in this poem and describe its effect on the reader.

METER: hendecasyllabic (see Catullus 5)

2 **ocellus**, -ī (*m*) (*diminutive*), little eye.

3 **digitus**, -ī (*m*), finger. **ōs, ōris** (*n*), mouth, lips. **siccus, -a, -um**, dry.

4 **sānē**, certainly, clearly, to be sure. **nimis**, especially, very, too. **ēlegāns, ēlegantis**, elegant, refined. *****lingua, -ae** (*f*), tongue, language.

5 **dēcoctor, dēcoctōris** (*m*), bankrupt spendthrift, playboy, rake. Many commentators identify the playboy as Mamurra, one of Caesar's generals, who had served in Gaul and whom Catullus attacks in other poems. The girl may be Ameana, his mistress. **amīca**: i.e., the **puella** of line 1. **Fōrmiānus, -a, -um**, from Formiae (a resort town south of Rome).

6 **tēn**: = **tēne**. What does the **-ne** signify? **prōvincia**: the Roman province of Cisalpine Gaul, where Ameana, if it is she, lived.

8 **saeclum**, -ī (*n*), generation, age. **īnsapiēns, īnsapientis**, tasteless, devoid of appreciation.

CATULLUS 43

"Hello, girl, with neither. . . ."

Catullus describes a girl whom many consider attractive and even compare to Lesbia.

1 Salvē, nec minimō puella nāsō
2 nec bellō pede nec nigrīs ocellīs
3 nec longīs digitīs nec ōre siccō
4 nec sānē nimis ēlegante linguā.
5 Dēcoctōris amīca Fōrmiānī,
6 tēn prōvincia nārrat esse bellam?
7 Tēcum Lesbia nostra comparātur?
8 Ō saeclum īnsapiēns et īnfacētum!

1. Specifically, what does Catullus find distasteful about the girl in lines 1–4?
2. In the first four lines Catullus employs *litotes*, a figure of speech in which a statement is made through the negation of its opposite, such as, "That was *no small* accomplishment." Point out this device and explain why it is effective. What other poetic device heightens the impact of these lines?
3. Compare line 5 to the other lines. How and why does Catullus draw attention to it?
4. What is the *tone* (the poet's attitude toward the subject matter) of the last four lines? What generalization does Catullus make in the last line? What has led him to this conclusion?
5. Why is Lesbia's name mentioned and not the names of the other two people? How might this poem give us a glimpse of what the poet found most attractive about Lesbia?
6. Ezra Pound (1885–1972), a modern poet who also found himself at odds with the taste and values of his time, translated this poem. How well does the translation convey the tone of the original? Where has Pound taken liberties? Explain the strange phrase, "vendor of cosmetics."

To Formianus' Young Lady Friend
   After Valerius Catullus

All Hail; young lady with a nose
   by no means too small,
With a foot unbeautiful,
   and with eyes that are not black,
With fingers that are not long, and with a mouth undry,
And with a tongue by no means too elegant,
You are the friend of Formianus, the vendor of cosmetics,
And they call you beautiful in the province,
And you are even compared to Lesbia.

O most unfortunate age!

METER: hendecasyllabic (see Catullus 5). The word **aureīs** (3) is scanned as two long syllables.

1 **vēr, vēris** (*n*), spring.   **ēgelidōs**: the prefix **ē**, from **ex**, here either strengthens the adjective **gelidus, -a, -um**, "cold," to mean "quite cool," or suggests the opposite, "with the chill off."   **tepōrēs, tepōrum** (*m pl*), warmth (i.e., "warm days"). Catullus may have tried to capture the many changes and contrasts of spring in the words **ēgelidōs ... tepōrēs**, an *oxymoron* (contradictory words used together): "chilly warm days." Another possible translation of the phrase is "warm days no longer chill."

2 **furor, furōris** (*m*), fury, rage, storminess.   **aequinoctiālis, -is, -e**, equinoctial (i.e., occurring at the spring equinox). Take with **caelī**.

3 *****iūcundus, -a, -um**, delightful, pleasant.   **Zephyrus, -ī** (*m*), Zephyr, west wind.   **silēscō, silēscere** (3), to become silent, quiet down. Verbs ending in **-scō**, such as **silēscō** and **vigēscō** (8), are called *inceptive*; they denote an action in its beginning stages. Why would inceptive verbs be appropriate for this poem?   **aura, -ae** (*f*), wind, breeze. **aureīs**: = **aurīs**.

4 **linquō, linquere** (3), **līquī**, to leave behind, abandon. **Liquantur**: what mood and construction?   **Phrygius, -a, -um**, Phrygian (referring to an area in central Asia Minor).

5 **Nicaea, -ae** (*f*), Nicaea (capital of Bithynia in northern Asia Minor).   **ūber, ūberis**, rich, fertile.   **aestuōsus, -a, -um**, hot, sweltering.

6 **clārus, -a, -um**, brilliant, famous.   **Asia, -ae** (*f*), Asia Minor.   **volēmus**: from **volō** (1). What mood and construction?

7 **praetrepidāns, praetrepidantis**, trembling in anticipation.   **aveō, avēre** (2), to wish, want, long to.   **vagor, vagārī** (1), **vagātus sum**, to wander, rush away, roam.

8 **studium, -i** (*n*), eagerness, enthusiasm.   **vigēscō, vigēscere** (3), to grow strong, come alive.

9 *****dulcis, -is, -e**, sweet.   **comes, comitis** (*m*), companion.   **coetus, -ūs** (*m*), group, company. **coetūs**: vocative plural.

10 **longē**, far. Take with **ā domō profectōs**.

11 **variē**, variously, "by different routes."   **reportant**: translate the compound verb literally.

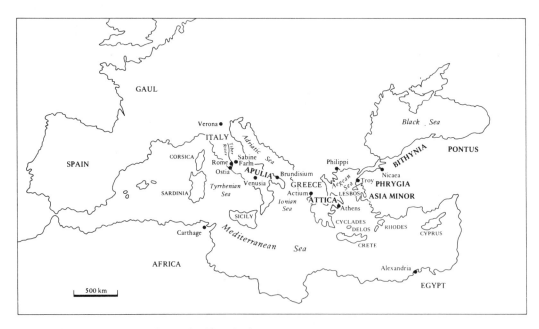

The Mediterranean area as it was in Cicero's time

CATULLUS 46

Spring Has Arrived.

How does this poem succeed in conveying the poet's eagerness for journeying home from the East and sorrow in saying goodbye to friends?

Iam vēr ēgelidōs refert tepōrēs,
iam caelī furor aequinoctiālis
iūcundīs Zephyrī silēscit aureīs.
Linquantur Phrygiī, Catulle, campī
5   Nicaeaeque ager ūber aestuōsae:
ad clārās Asiae volēmus urbēs.
Iam mēns praetrepidāns avet vagārī,
iam laetī studiō pedēs vigēscunt.
Ō dulcēs comitum valēte coetūs,
10 longē quōs simul ā domō profectōs
dīversae variē viae reportant.

1. **What do the first three lines of the poem celebrate and what feelings do they evoke? Lines 4–8? The last three lines?**

2. **Repetition of words, letters, and sounds is significant in this poem. Why is the word *iam* repeated four times? Words that have the letter *v* in them are central to the poem. Locate these words and describe the pattern that you see in their use. Find examples of *assonance* (close recurrence of similar vowel sounds) and *consonance* (close recurrence of similar consonant sounds).**

3. **Compare and contrast lines 1–2 with lines 7–8. How does the arrival of spring influence and mirror the poet's internal state of mind?**

4. **What does the use of proper names in lines 4–6 add to the poem?**

5. **The arrival of spring has served as a metaphor for many poets. Read the following excerpts from Chaucer's *The Canterbury Tales* and T. S. Eliot's *The Waste Land*. What aspects of spring and springtime activity do these two passages share with poem 46 of Catullus? How are the attitudes of the three poets toward spring similar and how are they different?**

As soon as April pierces to the root
The drought of March, and bathes each bud and shoot
Through every vein of sap with gentle showers
From whose engendering liquor spring the flowers;
When zephyrs have breathed softly all about
Inspiring every wood and field to sprout. . . .
Then off as pilgrims people long to go,
And palmers to set out for distant strands
And foreign shrines renowned in many lands.
(Geoffrey Chaucer, ca. 1340–1400)

April is the cruellest month, breeding
Lilacs out of the dead land, mixing
Memory and desire, stirring
Dull roots with spring rain.
(T. S. Eliot, 1888–1965)

1 *disertus, -a, -um, articulate, eloquent.   Disertissime: what form and case?
   Rōmulus, -ī (m), first king of Rome.   nepōs, nepōtis (m), grandson, descendant.
2 *quot, as many, however many.   fuēre: = fuērunt.   Marcus Tullius: Marcus Tullius
   Cicero (106–43 B.C.), Rome's greatest orator and a contemporary of Catullus.
3 post (adv.), later, afterwards, hereafter.
6 tantō . . . quantō (7), as much . . . as.
7 patrōnus, -ī (m), patron, defender. Supply es.

Disertissime Rōmulī nepōtum. . . .

CATULLUS 49

A Poem of "Thanks" to Cicero

Catullus expresses his thanks to Rome's greatest orator for a service about which we know nothing.

1   Disertissime Rōmulī nepōtum,
2   quot sunt quotque fuēre, Marce Tullī,
3   quotque post aliīs erunt in annīs,
4   grātiās tibi maximās Catullus
5   agit pessimus omnium poēta,
6   tantō pessimus omnium poēta,
7   quantō tū optimus omnium patrōnus.

1. *Irony* is a device by which a speaker or writer expresses one meaning but expects the audience to be aware of another, usually opposite, meaning. We rely on intonation, context, or verbal cues to help us detect the irony. On the surface, this is a very flattering poem of thanks to Cicero. What in the poem, however, may lead us to suspect irony on the part of Catullus?

2. The last line of the poem may be intentionally ambiguous since two meanings are possible. Is Cicero the best of all defenders or the best defender of everybody? What is the difference in meaning?

3. How well does the following imitation catch the possible irony of the original? Which English words are exaggerated and out of place in this show of gratitude? Which Latin words were out of place in the original?

(Imitated after Dining with Mr. Murray)

O Thou, of British orators the chief
That were, or are in being, or belief;
All eminence and goodness as thou art,
Accept the gratitude of Poet Smart,—
The meanest of the tuneful train as far,
As thou transcend'st the brightest at the bar.
        (Christopher Smart, 1722–1771)

METER: sapphic (named for the Greek poet Sappho. Horace uses this meter frequently; Catullus only twice. See Introduction, p. 1). The first three lines of each stanza repeat the same metrical pattern; the fourth, called an adonic, is different:

(3 lines) $- \smile - - - \| \smile \smile - \smile - \breve{}$

(1 line) $- \smile \smile - \breve{}$

In the first three lines of each stanza a caesura normally falls after the fifth syllable.

1 **Ille**: i.e., a man discussed further in lines 3–4. **mī**: take with **vidētur**.
2 **fās est**, it is permitted. The word **fās** often refers to what is permissible under divine law. **superāre**: supply **vidētur**. *__*dīvōs__: = **deōs**.
3 **adversus, -a, -um**, opposite. **identidem**, again and again, repeatedly.
5 **dulce**: = **dulciter**. **miserō**: take in agreement with **mihi** (6) as a dative of separation ("from . . ."). **quod**: "a situation which" (a summation of lines 1–4 and subject of **ēripit** in line 6). **omnīs**: = **omnēs**. In early Latin and in many of the poets, the accusative plural of i-stem nouns and adjectives often ends in **-īs**.
6 **sēnsus, -ūs** (*m*), sensation, feeling, (plural) consciousness. **simul**: supply **ac**.
7 *__**aspiciō, aspicere**__ (3), **aspexī, aspectum**, to catch sight of, behold, look at. **nihil . . . mī**: the full meaning of this is unclear, since line 8 has been lost in transmission. Can you think of a way to fill in the gap? **super**, over, left, remaining.
9 **torpeō, torpēre** (2), to become numb. **tenuis, -is, -e**, thin, fine. *__**artūs, -uum**__ (*m pl*), joints, limbs.
10 **dēmānō** (1), to flow down, penetrate. **sonitus, -ūs** (*m*), sound, noise. **suōpte**: "by their very own" (-**pte** intensifies the possessive adjective).
11 **tintinō** (1), to ring. *__**auris, auris**__ (*f*), ear. **geminus, -a, -um**, twin, double. Catullus uses a striking *transferred epithet* (an adjective used to describe one noun instead of another that it would normally modify) here. With what word does **geminā** agree grammatically? With what word does it agree in sense? **tegō, tegere** (3), **tēxī, tēctum**, to cover.
12 **lūmen, lūminis** (*n*), light, (plural) eyes.
13 *__**ōtium, -ī**__ (*n*), leisure, freedom from responsibility, idleness. **molestus, -a, -um**, annoying, bothersome. Note that the fourth syllable of this line is short.
14 **exsultō** (1), to rejoice, revel in. **nimium**, too much. **gestiō, gestīre** (4), **gestīvī**, to carry on, enjoy oneself, desire.
15 **prius** (*adv.*), before, previously.

6. **In the following poem by Shelley (1792–1822), what new elements have been added? What has been retained from Sappho? From Catullus?**

To Constantia Singing

My brain is wild, my breath comes quick,—
   The blood is listening in my frame,
And thronging shadows, fast and thick,
    Fall on my overflowing eyes:
My heart is quivering like a flame;
As morning dew, that in the sunbeam dies,
I am dissolved in these consuming ecstasies.

Catullus Translates a Poem from Sappho.

This poem is considered the first in the cycle of love poems to Lesbia.

> Ille mī pār esse deō vidētur,
> ille, sī fās est, superāre dīvōs,
> quī sedēns adversus identidem tē
>   spectat et audit
5 dulce rīdentem, miserō quod omnīs
> ēripit sēnsūs mihi: nam simul tē,
> Lesbia, aspexī, nihil est super mī
>   .   .   .   .
>
> lingua sed torpet, tenuis sub artūs
10 flamma dēmānat, sonitū suōpte
> tintinant aurēs, geminā teguntur
>   lūmina nocte.
> Ōtium, Catulle, tibī molestum est;
> ōtiō exsultās nimiumque gestīs;
15 ōtium et rēgēs prius et beātās
>   perdidit urbēs.

1. **This poem is a translation or adaptation of a Greek poem written by the female poet Sappho (ca. 620–ca. 550 B.C.). Here is a translation of Sappho's poem:**

> Fortunate as the gods he seems to me, that man who sits
>   opposite you, and listens nearby to your sweet voice
> And your lovely laughter; that, I vow, has set my heart
>   within my breast a-flutter. For when I look at you a
>   moment, then I have no longer power to speak,
> But my tongue keeps silence, straightway a subtle flame has
>   stolen beneath my flesh, with my eyes I see nothing, my
>   ears are humming,
> A cold sweat covers me, and a trembling seizes me all over,
>   I am paler than grass, I seem to be not far short of death. . . .
> But all must be endured, since. . . .
>
>   (translated by Denys Page)

2. **In Sappho's poem who are the three people? Give a specific account of the sensations Sappho feels in stanzas 3, 4, and 5.**

3. **If, in Catullus' translation, the word *tē* (3) refers to Lesbia, the woman with whom Catullus has fallen in love, who are the other two people? In the first three stanzas, where has Catullus changed the original? Why did he do so?**

4. **The initial placement and repetition of the word *ōtium* in the fourth stanza make this word significant. According to Catullus, what has *ōtium* been responsible for in the past? Why do you think it is *molestum* to Catullus? What in the past has *ōtium* allowed him, the poet and person, to indulge in? What are the consequences of *ōtium* both to great kings and cities and to small people (Catullus)?**

5. **The last stanza is not in Sappho's original, and there is some question as to whether or not it belongs to poem 51. Do you see a connection between it and the first three stanzas? Some commentators believe that the fourth stanza was added to poem 51 after the affair was over. If that is so, what possible comment on the first three stanzas did Catullus intend?**

METER: hendecasyllabic (see Catullus 5). In line 4, **ait** is scanned as two short syllables.

1 **nescio quem**: "someone or other." The indefinite pronoun **nesciō quis, nesciō quid** was initially a phrase that meant "I don't know who," "I don't know what." Note that only the **quis, quid** part declines. **corōna, -ae** (*f*), garland, circle (of people), audience, crowd. It was a common sight in Rome to see a circle of bystanders gathered in a **basilica** (Roman law court) to watch a trial.

2 ***mīrificus, -a, -um**, wonderful, marvelous. **Vatīniānus, -a, -um**, of Vatinius (Publius Vatinius, whom Calvus was prosecuting).

3 **crīmen, crīminis** (*n*), crime, charge. **Calvus, -ī** (*m*), Gaius Licinius Calvus (82–ca. 47 B.C.), an orator, poet, and close friend of Catullus. **explicō** (1), to explicate, explain, set forth. **explicāsset:** = **explicāvisset:** what mood, tense, and construction?

4 **ait**, (he) says. **haec:** "the following words."

5 **salapūtium disertum:** "what an eloquent little squirt." **salapūtium, -ī** (*n*), little man. Calvus was apparently short.

METER: elegiac couplet, a Greek variation on the dactylic hexameter, the meter used for epic and some long poems, such as Homer's *Iliad*, Vergil's *Aeneid*, and poem 64 of Catullus. The elegiac couplet was used for a variety of purposes, including drinking songs, epitaphs, love poems, lamentations, and reflections. The origin of the words *elegiac* and *elegy* is uncertain, but it is clear that the elegiac meter was not confined to serious subjects. The elegiac couplet consists of a line in dactylic hexameter and a pentameter, the latter of which is dactylic except for the third and sixth feet, where only the long syllable of the dactyl remains. The first four feet of the hexameter line may be either dactylic ($-\smile\smile$) or spondaic ($--$); the fifth foot is regularly a dactyl, and the sixth a spondee or trochee ($-\stackrel{\smile}{-}$). In the pentameter line, the first two feet may be dactylic or spondaic, but the fourth and fifth feet are always dactylic.

Hexameter: $-\stackrel{\smile}{\smile}|-\stackrel{\smile}{\smile}|-\stackrel{\smile}{\smile}|-\stackrel{\smile}{\smile}|-\stackrel{\smile}{\smile}|-\stackrel{\smile}{}$

Pentameter: $-\stackrel{\smile}{\smile}|-\stackrel{\smile}{\smile}|-\|-\smile\smile|-\smile\smile|\stackrel{\smile}{}$

A caesura may fall in the second, third, or fourth foot of the hexameter. The pentameter line has no regular caesura but instead a *diaeresis* (word-end between metrical feet here frequently coinciding with a pause in the sense) after the third foot.

1 **Nūllī . . . mālle:** translate in this order: **mea mulier dīcit sē nūllī nūbere mālle.** Explain the construction of each infinitive in this line.
 nūbō, nūbere (3), **nūpsī, nūptum** (+ *dat.*), to get married to.

2 **sē:** i.e., the **mulier** mentioned in line 1. **petat:** what mood and tense? This is the first half (protasis) of a future less vivid condition. How is the protasis of this type of conditional sentence translated?

3 **quod:** place **quod** after **sed** and translate: "but what a woman says. . . ." This clause is the object of **scrībere** in line 4. **cupidus, -a, -um**, desiring, lusting.
 ***amāns, amantis** (*m*), lover.

4 **oportet, oportēre** (2), **oportuit** (+ *infinitive*), it is necessary, one ought.

CATULLUS 53

An Amusing Incident at the Law Court

What is the dramatic situation of this short poem? What did Catullus find humorous?

1 Rīsī nescio quem modo ē corōnā,
2 quī, cum mīrificē Vatīniāna
3 meus crīmina Calvus explicāsset,
4 admīrāns ait haec manūsque tollēns:
5 "dī magnī, salapūtium disertum!"

1. Compare this poem to poem 49. What are the clues in both poems that Catullus was critical of the excessive rhetorical styles (verbal and theatrical) of certain lawyers and orators?
2. We know that Cicero and Calvus often faced each other in trials. What is the difference in tone between poem 49 to Cicero and poem 53 on Calvus?

CATULLUS 70

Words, Words, Words!

This is one of several poems in which Catullus tries to analyze the failure of his love affair with Lesbia. What is the theme or central idea of this short poem? What is the tone?

1 Nūllī sē dīcit mulier mea nūbere mālle
2   quam mihi, nōn sī sē Iuppiter ipse petat.
3 Dīcit: sed mulier cupidō quod dīcit amantī,
4   in ventō et rapidā scrībere oportet aquā.

1. At the center of this poem is the poet's use of irony. Are we to believe that the woman is saying one thing but meaning another (*rhetorical irony*) or is she unaware of the real significance of her words as the poet and audience understand them (*dramatic irony*)? Which irony do you feel that the poet is using? Defend your answer with reference to this and other poems of Catullus.
2. Find examples of repetition and hyperbole. Why are they effective devices in this poem?
3. A fragment from Sophocles (ca. 496–406 B.C.) reads: "I write the oath of a woman onto water." Why are winds and waters such fitting receptacles for empty promises?
4. Compare poem 70 with the following translation of an epigram by the Greek poet Callimachus (ca. 305–ca. 240 B.C.; see Introduction, p. 1). How has each poet treated the same theme differently? What is the difference in tone?

   Callignotus swore to Ionis that he would hold
   neither man nor woman dearer than her.
   He swore: the truth is that love's oaths
   do not enter the ears of the immortals.
   Now he burns for a man, while of the poor girl,
   as of the Megarians, there is no word or record.

METER: elegiac couplet (see Catullus 70).

1 **Dīcēbās**: translate lines 1–2 in the following order: **Dīcēbās quondam tē Catullum sōlum nōsse nec (tē) Iovem prae mē tenēre velle.** **nōsse**: = **nōvisse.**

2 **prae** (+ *abl.*), instead of, before.

2 **Iovem**: from **Iuppiter, Iovis** (*m*).

3 *****dīligō, dīligere** (3), **dīlēxī, dīlēctum**, to esteem, cherish, love. **nōn tantum**, not only. **ut vulgus amīcam**: supply **dīligit.** What does **ut** mean when it is not followed by a subjunctive?

4 **gnātus, -ī** (*m*), son. **gener, generī** (*m*), son-in-law.

5 **impēnsus, -a, -um**, strong, vehement, grievous. What degree of the adverb is **impēnsius**? *****ūrō, ūrere** (3), **ussī, ūstum**, to burn, (passive) be on fire (with love).

6 *****multō . . . vīlior**: "cheaper by much," "much cheaper." Adjectives in the ablative, such as **multō** and **parvō**, can be used with the comparative to express the degree of difference. **vīlis, -is, -e**, cheap, common. **levis, -is, -e**, light, of little worth, fickle, contemptible.

7 **quī** (*adv.*), how. *****potis, -is, -e**, possible. **Quī potis est**: "How is this possible?" "How can this be?" **amantem**: from the noun **amāns, amantis** (*m*). *****tālis, -is, -e**, such, of this kind.

8 *****bene velle**, to be fond of, like, respect.

. . . *sed pater ut gnātōs dīligit et generōs.*

CATULLUS 72

"Now I know you."

In this poem Catullus probes deeper into his complex feelings for Lesbia.

1　Dīcēbās quondam sōlum tē nōsse Catullum,
2　　Lesbia, nec prae mē velle tenēre Iovem.
3　Dīlēxī tum tē nōn tantum ut vulgus amīcam,
4　　sed pater ut gnātōs dīligit et generōs.
5　Nunc tē cognōvī: quārē etsī impēnsius ūror,
6　　multō mī tamen es vīlior et levior.
7　Qūi potis est, inquis? Quod amantem iniūria tālis
8　　cōgit amāre magis, sed bene velle minus.

1. Compare the opening couplet of this poem to the opening of poem 70. What are the similarities? What does the change of tense from *dīcit* to *dīcēbās* suggest?
2. What do you notice about word placement in the first couplet? Where are the important words?
3. What was the nature of the poet's affection for Lesbia according to the second couplet? What will become of his affection by the end of the poem?
4. Describe the bond that existed between a Roman father and his son, and between a Roman father and his son-in-law. Why does Catullus single out these bonds for comparison with that between a crowd and its mistress (3–4)?
5. The verb *cognōvī* (5) recalls *nōsse* in line 1. Both verbs may be used to describe intellectual as well as carnal knowing. Explain the meaning of *nunc tē cognōvī* in each sense.
6. What dilemma does Catullus face in lines 5–6 and how does he account for it in lines 7–8? What is the *iniūria*? As you understand it from this poem, describe clearly the difference between the expressions *dīlēxī, ūror, amāre,* and *bene velle*.
7. How does Catullus use time effectively in organizing this poem? Be specific in your answer.

: elegiac couplet (see Catullus 70). Line 6 is metrically unusual. How and why?

1 **dē quōquam**: "from anyone." **velle**: **velle** and **putāre** (2) are complementary infinitives after **dēsine**. Explain the use of the infinitives **merērī**, **fierī**, and **posse** (1–2). **mereor**, **merērī** (2), **meritus sum**, to earn, deserve. **bene merērī**, to be rightfully entitled to.

2 *__pius__, **-a**, **-um**, dutiful, grateful.

3 *__ingrātus__, **-a**, **-um**, unappreciated, thankless. **nihil . . . prōdest** (4): "it is not profitable to have done anything with kindness." **benignē**, kindly, with kindness.

4 **prōsum**, **prōdesse** (*irreg.*), **prōfuī**, to profit, be of use. **immō**, on the contrary. **taedet**, it is wearisome, tiring. What is the antecedent of "it"? **obsum**, **obesse** (*irreg.*), **obfuī** (+ *dat.*), to get in the way, be harmful.

5 **ut mihi**: "as it is to me." **quem nēmō . . . quam** (6) **. . . quī**: "whom no one . . . than he who. . . ." **acerbus**, **-a**, **-um**, sharp, painful. What does the ending on the words **gravius** and **acerbius** indicate? **urgeō**, **urgēre** (2), **ursī**, to press, distress, vex.

6 **ūnicus**, **-a**, **-um**, only. **habeō**, **habēre** (2), **habuī**, **habitum**, to have, hold, consider.

: elegiac couplet (see Catullus 70).

1 **dēdūcō**, **dēdūcere** (3), **dēdūxī**, **dēductum**, to lead down, drag down. **culpa**, **-ae** (*f*), fault, infidelity.

2 **officiō . . . suō**: "by its own commitment," "by its own devotion." **ipsa**: i.e., **mēns**.

3 **ut**: does this introduce a purpose or result clause here? How do you know? **queat**: present subjunctive, "it is possible (for me)," "I am able." **tibi**: dative with **bene velle**. **sī optima fīās**: what type of conditional clause? Compare **omnia sī faciās** (4).

CATULLUS 73

Ingratitude Everywhere

What are some possibilities for the grievance at the heart of this poem?

1 Dēsine dē quōquam quicquam bene velle merērī
2   aut aliquem fierī posse putāre pium.
3 Omnia sunt ingrāta, nihil fēcisse benignē
4   prōdest, immō etiam taedet obestque magis;
5 ut mihi, quem nēmō gravius nec acerbius urget,
6   quam modo quī mē ūnum atque ūnicum amīcum habuit.

1. The words *merērī* (1), *pium* (2), *(in)grāta* (3), *benignē* (3), and *prōdest* (4) refer to traditional values in Roman society. These values put great store in a network of mutual loyalties and gratitudes between individuals, the state, and the gods. What radical proposal(s) is Catullus making in this poem?
2. The word *taedet* in line 4 is difficult to translate. What does Catullus mean by the word in this context? Defend your choice of translation.
3. What *imagery* (use of descriptive language to represent people or objects, often appealing to our senses) does Catullus use in this poem? How many nouns can you find? Of what significance are your findings? From what does this poem draw its power?
4. Where else in the poems you have read has Catullus generalized from a particular experience and drawn large conclusions? Have you encountered this tendency before, perhaps in other writers or from among people you know? Where? How do you explain this very human trait?

CATULLUS 75

The Love-Hate Deepens.

Catullus admits in this short poem that personal reflection and analysis have worsened his condition.

1 Hūc est mēns dēducta tuā, mea Lesbia, culpā
2   atque ita sē officiō perdidit ipsa suō,
3 ut iam nec bene velle queat tibi, sī optima fīās,
4   nec dēsistere amāre, omnia sī faciās.

1. Catullus has put strong emphasis on the opening word, *hūc*. To what state of mind does *hūc* refer? How does the compound verb *dēdūcere* strengthen the assertion?
2. In lines 1–2, what is Catullus claiming he did and that Lesbia did not do? Consider the words *culpā* and *officiō* in your answer. What is the consequence of his action according to line 2?
3. In your own words state what the last two lines say. Is the word *omnia* meant to be positive or negative? Compare this couplet to the last couplet of poem 72. What more desperate note has been sounded here?
4. Read the poem in meter. How many elisions do you find? Why are the ones in line 4 so effective?

METER: elegiac couplet (see Catullus 70). How is the fifth foot of line 15 unusual? Why? What emphasis is brought to the word **pervincendum**? No elision occurs between **extrēmam** and **iam** in line 18.

1 **Sīqua**: the first four lines set up the general conditions upon which the sadly worded conclusion of lines 5–8 is built. Translate lines 1–4 in this order: **Sīqua voluptās est hominī recordantī benefacta priōra, cum cōgitat sē esse pium, nec (sē) violāsse sanctam fidem, nec (sē) abūsum (esse) nūmine dīvum (= deōrum) ad fallendōs hominēs (in) foedere nūllō (= ūllō). . . . sīqua: = sī qua**, if any. **Sīqua . . . voluptās est** (2): "If there is any pleasure." **recordor, recordārī** (1), **recordātus sum**, to remember. Participles of deponent verbs are normally active in meaning. **recordantī . . . hominī** (2): dative of possession.
benefactum, -ī (n), kindness, good deed.

3 **nec . . . nec**: "and has not . . . nor." *****sānctus, -a, -um**, sacred, holy, hallowed. **violō** (1), to violate, break. **violāsse**: = **violāvisse**. Why is an infinitive used here? What tense is it? *****foedus, foederis** (n), contract, pact, agreement.

4 **ad fallendōs . . . hominēs**: what form is **fallendōs**? How do you translate it with **ad**? **nūmen, nūminis** (n), divinity, power. What case is **nūmine** and why? **abūtor, abūtī** (3), **abūsus sum** (+ abl.), to abuse, misuse.

5 **multa**: translate lines 5–6 in this order: **multa gaudia, parāta ex hōc ingrātō amōre, Catulle, in longā aetāte tibi manent. parō** (1), to prepare, furnish, acquire, obtain. **in longā aetāte**: "in the long years ahead," "for the remainder of your life."

6 **gaudium, -ī** (n), joy, pleasure.

7 **quaecumque**: "whatever things." **bene**: take with **dīcere** and **facere** (8).

9 **Omnia . . . mentī**: translate in this order: **Omnia, quae periērunt, crēdita (sunt) ingrātae mentī** (i.e., Lesbia's). **crēdō, crēdere** (3), **crēdidī, crēditum** (+ dat.), to believe, entrust.

10 **amplius**, more, further. *****excruciō** (1), to torture, torment. **excruciēs**: deliberative subjunctive.

11 **Quīn tū**: "Why don't you . . . ? **animō**: = **in animō**. **offirmō** (1), to be firm, be determined, grow strong. **istinc**, from there, "from where you are" (i.e., from a weak and dismal state of mind).

12 **dīs invītīs**: "if the gods are unwilling" (i.e., to let Catullus suffer) or "because the gods are unwilling" (i.e., to let the affair be a happy one). Are there other possibilities? Which interpretation do you prefer? Why?

14 **quālubet**, in any way possible. **efficiō, efficere** (3), **effēcī, effectum**, to accomplish, carry out. Why is a subjunctive used here?

15 **haec**: feminine singular in place of the neuter **hoc**, by attraction to the gender of **salūs**. **hōc**: neuter nominative singular; sometimes, as here, the o is regarded as long. The four demonstratives in lines 14–16 refer to **longum subitō dēpōnere amōrem** (13). **pervincō, pervincere** (3), **pervīcī, pervictum**, to bring about, accomplish. **est . . . pervincendum**: what form and construction?

16 **id . . . pote**: supply **est**.

17 **sī vestrum est** (+ infinitive.): "if it is characteristic of you," "if it is within you." **vestrum**: genitive of **vōs**.
misereor, miserērī (2), **miseritus sum**, to have pity, have mercy.

18 **extrēmus, -a, -um**, final, last-minute.

20 **pestis, pestis** (f), disease, plague. **perniciēs, -ēī** (f), destruction, ruin. **mihi**: here, a dative of separation. In line 21, take it as dative of reference or possession.

21 **subrēpō, subrēpere** (3), **subrepsī, subreptum**, to crawl, creep down. **īmus, -a, -um**, deepest. **torpor, torpōris** (m), numbness.

22 **pectus, pectoris** (n), chest, heart, soul. *****laetitia, -ae** (f), gladness, joy.

23 **illud . . . ut . . . illa**: "the following . . . , that she. . . ." **contrā** (adv.), in return. Take with **dīligat**.

24 **quod**, (something) that. **potis**: = **pote**. **pudīcus, -a, -um**, virtuous, honorable. **velit**: what mood and tense?

25 **optō** (1), to wish, want. **taeter, taetra, taetrum**, offensive, revolting, foul. **morbus, -ī** (m), disease, sickness.

26 **pietās, pietātis** (f), dutifulness, devotion.

CATULLUS 76

An Urgent Plea for a Quid Pro Quo

*Finding no relief from the pain of his physical attachment to Lesbia and
from his equally strong abhorrence of her behavior, Catullus appeals to
the gods for salvation.*

Sīqua recordantī benefacta priōra voluptās
   est hominī, cum sē cōgitat esse pium,
nec sānctam violāsse fidem, nec foedere nūllō
   dīvum ad fallendōs nūmine abūsum hominēs,
5   multa parāta manent in longā aetāte, Catulle,
   ex hōc ingrātō gaudia amōre tibi.
Nam quaecumque hominēs bene cuiquam aut dīcere possunt
   aut facere, haec ā tē dictaque factaque sunt.
Omnia quae ingrātae periērunt crēdita mentī.
10   Quārē iam tē cūr amplius excruciēs?
Quīn tū animō offirmās atque istinc tē ipse redūcis,
   et dīs invītīs dēsinis esse miser?
Difficile est longum subitō dēpōnere amōrem,
   difficile est, vērum hoc quālubet efficiās:
15   ūna salūs haec est, hōc est tibi pervincendum,
   hoc faciās, sīve id nōn pote sīve pote.
Ō dī, sī vestrum est miserērī, aut sī quibus umquam
   extrēmam iam ipsā in morte tulistis opem,
mē miserum aspicite et, sī vītam pūriter ēgī,
20   ēripite hanc pestem perniciemque mihi,
quae mihi subrēpēns īmōs ut torpor in artūs
   expulit ex omnī pectore laetitiās.
Nōn iam illud quaerō, contrā mē ut dīligat illa,
   aut, quod nōn potis est, esse pudīca velit:
25   ipse valēre optō et taetrum hunc dēpōnere morbum.
   Ō dī, reddite mī hoc prō pietāte meā.

1. Under what conditions, according to Catullus, should a person find pleasure in remembering *benefacta priōra* (1)?
2. What sad irony is suggested by the placement of the word *gaudia* in line 6?
3. What claim does the poet make for himself in lines 7–8?
4. From what aspect(s) of Roman life are the vocabulary and *diction* (the choice and arrangement of words to fit the subject matter) of lines 1–9 drawn? Explain the significance of your answer.
5. In line 9 the word *crēdita* is an allusion to financial investment. What is Catullus saying about his investment in Lesbia?
6. Lines 13–26 explore the idea of love as a disease. Cite examples of anaphora, repetition, alliteration, assonance, line framing, hendiadys, *simile* (a comparison between two things, expressed by the words *like* or *as*), and *metaphor* (an implicit comparison between two things without the words *like* or *as*) that Catullus uses to paint his desperate situation and the extent of the disease. How do the individual devices reinforce the urgency of the situation?
7. What is Catullus' state of mind as he makes his final wish in lines 23–26? What does the word *pietāte* look back to earlier in the poem?

1 **praesente virō**: "while her husband is present."
   *****mala . . . dīcit**: this and **dīcit . . . male** (Catullus 92) are equivalent to **maledīcō, maledīcere** (3), **maledīxī, maledictum** (+ *dat.*), to curse, heap abuse upon.

2 **haec**: i.e., the verbal abuse mentioned in line 1. Explain why **haec**, not **hoc**, is used here. Compare the use of **haec** in line 15 of Catullus 76.   **illī fatuō**: i.e., Lesbia's husband.   **fatuus, -a, -um**, foolish.   **laetitia**: predicate nominative.

3 **mūlus, -ī** (*m*), mule.   **nostrī**: genitive of **nōs**.   **oblītus, -a, -um** (+ *gen.*), forgetful of.   *****taceō, tacēre** (2), **tacuī, tacitum**, to be quiet.   **tacēret**: the subject is Lesbia. What mood and tense are **tacēret** here and **esset** in line 4? What type of conditional sentence is this?

4 **sānus, -a, -um**, sane, rational, "in her right mind."   **banniō, gannīre** (4), to snarl.   **obloquor, obloquī** (3), **oblocūtus sum**, to interrupt, insist upon speaking.

5 **meminī, meminisse** (*perfect in form, present in meaning*), to remember.   **quae . . . rēs**: a parenthetical remark that looks ahead to **īrāta est** (6); translate idiomatically, "and the following fact. . . ."
   ācer, ācris, ācre, sharp, revealing. How do you translate **multō** when it is used with a comparative adjective?

6 **Hōc est**: "That is. . . ."   **Hōc**: nominative singular, with the o pronounced as a long vowel.

Lesbia mī praesente virō mala plūrima dīcit.

34

CATULLUS 83

Lesbia's Stinging Words Are Not What They Seem.

Catullus lays out before us the logic of love and the rules by which we can read the symptoms of this love. What in Lesbia's behavior leads Catullus to the conclusion at the end of the poem?

1 Lesbia mī praesente virō mala plūrima dīcit;
2   haec illī fatuō maxima laetitia est.
3 Mūle, nihil sentīs? Sī nostrī oblīta tacēret,
4   sāna esset: nunc quod gannit et obloquitur,
5 nōn sōlum meminit, sed, quae multō ācrior est rēs,
6   īrāta est. Hōc est, ūritur et loquitur.

1. Describe the situation in the first couplet. Why does Catullus call the husband a mule in the second couplet?
2. Catullus pays great attention to the design of his poems. You can often divide the poems into symmetrical units and see the development of his thoughts. In this poem, each couplet is a unit and part of a progression that builds up to the final words, *ūritur et loquitur.* Trace this progression.
3. How does the contrary-to-fact condition in lines 3–4 strengthen the conviction stated in lines 5–6?
4. In terms of love and the emotions of love, what special meaning might *sāna* (4), *īrāta* (6), and *ūritur* (6) have? Why do you think there are so many references to speech in this poem (*dīcit, tacēret, gannit, obloquitur,* and *loquitur*)?

1 **Chommoda**: this is the first of three words in the poem that Arrius mispronounces by using an inappropriate Greek aspiration (the addition of a breath or *h* sound at the beginning of a word) in order to appear learned. **Commoda** (*n pl*, "advantages") becomes **chommoda** in his mouth. In your translation, try to imitate this humorous affectation or put the three aspirated words in quotation marks.
    sī quandō, if ever, whenever (+ subjunctive).   **vellet**: from what verb? What is the tense of the subjunctive here?

2 **īnsidiās Arrius hīnsidiās**: copy the pattern of **Chommoda . . . dīcere** (1–2) when you translate this.   **Arrius, -ī** (*m*), possibly Quintus Arrius, an orator of whom Cicero thought very little.

3 **mīrificē**: take with **esse locūtum**.

4 **quantum poterat**: "with as much effort as he could."

5 **sīc**, thus, in the same way.   **avunculus, -ī** (*m*), mother's brother, uncle.

6 **avus, -ī** (*m*), grandfather.   **avia, -ae** (*f*), grandmother.

7 **Hōc**: i.e., Arrius. What construction is **hōc missō**?   **requiēscō, requiēscere** (3), **requiēvī, requiētum**, to rest, find relief.   **requiērant**: = **requiēverant**.   **omnibus**: dative of possession ("everyone's") or reference ("for all concerned").

8 **audībant**: = **audiēbant**.   **eadem haec**: supply **verba** (i.e., the words **commoda** and **īnsidiae**).   **lēnis, -is, -e**, soft, gentle.   **leviter**: "lightly," "without aspiration."

9 **sibi**: dative of reference.   **postillā**, afterwards, after that time.

10 **nūntius**: sometimes an indirect statement is introduced through a reference to speech, as here; i.e., "a message is brought, that. . . ."

11 **Īonius, -a, -um**, Ionian (referring to the Ionian Sea off the west coast of Greece).   **flūctus, -ūs** (*m*), wave.   **illūc**, to there, there.   **īsset**: relative and temporal clauses inside indirect statements take the subjunctive.   **īsset**: = **iisset**. From what verb is **īsset**, and what tense is it?

Chommoda dīcēbat. . . .

36

CATULLUS 84

Arrius' Attempts at Learned Eloquence Have a Chilling Effect Wherever He Goes.

Chommoda dīcēbat, sī quandō commoda vellet
    dīcere, et īnsidiās Arrius hīnsidiās,
et tum mīrificē spērābat sē esse locūtum,
    cum quantum poterat dīxerat hīnsidiās.
5 Crēdō, sīc māter, sīc līber avunculus eius,
    sīc māternus avus dīxerat atque avia.
Hōc missō in Syriam requiērant omnibus aurēs:
    audībant eadem haec lēniter et leviter,
nec sibi postillā metuēbant tālia verba,
10   cum subitō affertur nūntius horribilis:
Īoniōs flūctūs, postquam illūc Arrius īsset,
    iam nōn Īoniōs esse sed Hīoniōs.

1. How does Catullus use the order and placement of words to highlight Arrius' humorous mispronunciations? A *chiasmus* is an arrangement of pairs of words in opposite order within a line or between lines; for example, "The cat jumped in, out jumped the mouse." Find the chiasmus in lines 1–2.

2. What do we learn about Arrius in lines 3–4? Compare this behavior to that described in lines 15–17 of poem 22 on Suffenus. What is the similarity? What is the poet's attitude toward this behavior?

3. Why does Catullus mention Arrius' family in lines 5–6? Discuss the possible *connotations* (positive or negative associations that a word may have) of the word *līber* (5) in this context?

4. "The humor of the poem is found particularly in the last line where the jest is double-edged: on the formal side, because terms applicable to wind and weather conditions were used in current grammatical study for phenomena including aspiration (e.g., *lēnis, levis, adspīrō, spīritus, asper*) and, more uproariously, because Arrius' aspiration added to the storminess of the Adriatic crossing." (*Roman Lyric Poetry*, p. 228) Describe in your own words the humor that the authors McKay and Shepherd detect in the final lines of the poem. There is an additional pun in the word *horribilis* (10), the root of which means "to bristle," "to be rough." Explain this pun in light of the quotation.

5. Catullus employs a variety of words for speaking and hearing in this poem. Find examples.

6. Here is an Anglicized version of Arrius. What is the particularly British mistake in pronunciation that Sir 'Arry makes? Which of the two poems do you prefer? Why?

Sir 'Arry, though lately created a knight,
Is unable to order his "h's" aright.
He expounds the wise views of "a man of haffairs"
Or explains " 'ow 'e 'ates haristocracy's hairs."
(To his mother, nee 'Awkins, he owes, I expect,
This unpleasant, invincible vocal defect.)
His victims had looked for a respite at least
While Sir 'Arry is occupied "doin' the Heast."
But alas for our hopes! You've not heard the news? What?
Sir 'Arry finds "Hindia 'ellishly 'ot."

                             (Anonymous)

METER: elegiac couplet (see Catullus 70). Note the short *o* in **nescio** (2).

1 **ōdī, odisse** (*perfect in form, present in meaning*), to hate. **quārē**, why, for what
   reason. **Quārē id faciam**: object of **requīris**. **faciam**: why subjunctive? **fortasse**,
   perhaps. **requīrō, requīrere** (3), **requīsīvī, requīsītum**, to ask.
2 **fierī**: infinitive in an indirect statement after **sentiō**; supply **id** as subject of the
   infinitive.

Nescio, sed fierī sentiō et excrucior.

38

CATULLUS 85

I Hate and I Love.

What is Catullus admitting here that he did not admit in poems 72 and 75?

1 Ōdī et amō. Quārē id faciam, fortasse requīris?
2   Nescio, sed fierī sentiō et excrucior.

1. **Read the poem aloud and in meter. How many elisions can you find and what is their effect?**
2. **Is the verb *ōdisse* (1) opposite in meaning to *amāre* (1) or to *bene velle*, as used in poems 72 and 75? Defend your answer.**
3. **What is the antecedent of *id* (1)?**
4. **Who is the "you" of *requīris*?**
5. **Explain what Catullus means by the two phrases *id faciam* (1) and *(id) fierī sentiō* (2).**
6. **How many verbs are there in this couplet? How many nouns and adjectives can you find? What is the importance of your discovery?**
7. **This has been a popular poem for performance and translation. Grade the following versions on their faithfulness to the original, their success in conveying the tone and sentiment, and their simplicity of expression. Be ready to justify your grading.**

> I hate, and yet I love thee too;
> How can that be? I know not how;
> Only that so it is I know;
> And feel with torment that 'tis so.
>   (Abraham Cowley, 1667)

> I hate and love. Why? You may ask but
> It beats me. I feel it done to me, and ache.
>   (Ezra Pound)

> I hate and I love. And if you ask me how,
> I do not know: I only feel it, and I'm torn in two.
>   (Peter Whigham)

> I HATE and love.
>   And if you ask me why,
> I have no answer, but I discern,
> can feel, my senses rooted in eternal torture.
>   (Horace Gregory)

> Of course I hate what I love, and can't explain,
> for how is one to syllogize his pain?
>   (Gary Wills)

METER: elegiac couplet (see Catullus 70).

1 **Quīntia, -ae** (*f*), a woman whom Catullus is comparing to Lesbia.
****fōrmōsus, -a, -um**, beautiful, gorgeous. **longus, -a, -um**, tall.

2 **rēctus, -a, -um,** (of posture) upright, stately. **singula, -ōrum** (*n pl*), individual features. **cōnfiteor, cōnfitērī** (2), **cōnfessus sum**, to confess, admit.

3 **Tōtum ... negō:** "I deny that all that (i.e., lines 1–2) is '**fōrmōsa.**' " The word **fōrmōsa** is quoted from line 1 and is grammatically unaffected by the indirect statement.
venustās, venustātis (*f*), charm, attractiveness.

4 **mīca, -ae** (*f*), grain, flicker.

5 **cum ... tum** (6), both ... and, not only ... but also. **pulcerrima:** = **pulcherrima.**

6 **omnibus:** "from all women." **omnīs:** = **omnēs.**
surripiō, surripere (3), **surripuī, surreptum**, to steal.

Lesbia ... omnibus ūna omnīs surripuit Venerēs.

CATULLUS 86

A "Beauty" Contest

*Why do the many find Quintia **fōrmōsa**? Why does Catullus disagree?*
*Why is Lesbia **fōrmōsa**?*

1   Quīntia fōrmōsa est multīs. Mihi candida, longa,
2   rēcta est: haec ego sīc singula cōnfiteor.
3   Tōtum illud fōrmōsa negō: nam nūlla venustās,
4   nūlla in tam magnō est corpore mīca salis.
5   Lesbia fōrmōsa est, quae cum pulcerrima tōta est,
6   tum omnibus ūna omnīs surripuit Venerēs.

1. Does Catullus distinguish between the adjectives *fōrmōsus* and *pulcher*? If so, how?
2. Examine the placement of the word *fōrmōsa* in each of the three couplets. What do you discover?
3. Where in the poem does Catullus deliberately place words in a special order to set himself and his values against society and its values?
4. What does Catullus mean by the plural *omnīs . . . Venerēs* in line 6? What relation does that phrase have to *nūlla venustās* in line 3?
5. Compare poem 86 to poem 43. What are the similarities and differences between the two poems?

METER: elegiac couplet (see Catullus 70).

1 **tantum**: take after **vērē** (2) and translate **tantum quantum** together, "as much as," "to the extent that." Do the same with **tanta** and **quanta** in lines 3–4.

   amātam: supply **esse**. Why is an infinitive used here? What tense and voice is it?

3 **ūllō . . . foedere**: = **in ūllō foedere**.

4 **in amōre tuō**: "in my love for you."   **reperta . . . est**: the subject is **fidēs**.

METER: elegiac couplet (see Catullus 70).

2 **Lesbia . . . amat**: translate in this order: **dispeream nisi Lesbia mē amat**.   ***dispereō**, **disperīre** (*irreg.*), **disperiī**, to be ruined, perish, die. **dispeream**: what mood and construction?

3 **Quō signō?**: "By what sign (do I know that she loves me)?"   **sunt totidem mea**: "my circumstances (or signs) are entirely the same," "it's the same for me."

   dēprecor, **dēprecārī** (1), **dēprecātus sum**, to wish someone away, try to get rid of, rebuke.

4 **assiduē**, continually, all the time.

CATULLUS 87

A Love Unparalleled

What aspect of love is Catullus discussing in the first couplet? In the second couplet? How has Catullus given the second couplet more emphasis? Why?

1 Nūlla potest mulier tantum sē dīcere amātam
2   vērē, quantum ā mē Lesbia amāta mea est.
3 Nūlla fidēs ūllō fuit umquam foedere tanta,
4   quanta in amōre tuō ex parte reperta mea est.

1. Where does Catullus use *interlocked word order* (an arrangement of two pairs of words so that one word of each pair is between the words of the other in an *abab* pattern, e.g., *Catullus candidam amat puellam*), repetition, alliteration, assonance, consonance, and hyperbole in this poem?
2. Which lines have elisions? What is their effect?
3. With what other poem(s) of Catullus has Walter Savage Landor (1775–1864) joined poem 87 in the following translation? Why did Landor join the poems together?

Love's Madness

None could ever say that she,
Lesbia! was so loved by me;
Never, all the world around,
Faith so true as mine was found.
If no longer it endures,

(Would it did!) the fault is yours.
I can never think again
Well of you: I try in vain.
But, be false, do what you will,
Lesbia! I must love you still.

CATULLUS 92

How Do I Know She Loves Me?

In this poem, as in poem 83, Catullus manages to read Lesbia's behavior in a paradoxical or contradictory way. What is the paradoxical proposition in the first couplet and how does he prove his assertion in the second couplet?

1 Lesbia mī dīcit semper male nec tacet umquam
2   dē mē: Lesbia mē dispeream nisi amat.
3 Quō signō? Quia sunt totidem mea: dēprecor illam
4   assiduē, vērum dispeream nisi amō.

1. In poem 83, Catullus was addressing Lesbia's husband. Whom is he addressing in this poem?
2. What is the new element in this poem that was not present in poem 83?
3. What may be wrong with the poet's reasoning? Why is it a dangerous mistake for anyone to make?
4. For what reasons might any two lovers verbally abuse each other as Catullus and Lesbia seem to be doing?

METER: elegiac couplet (see Catullus 70).

1 **Sī quicquam . . . grātum . . . potest** (2): "If anything pleasing . . . can. . . ."
 *****mūtus, -a, -um**, mute, silent. **mūtīs . . . sepulcrīs**: dative with **grātum** and **acceptum**.
 acceptus, -a, -um (+ *dat.*), welcome. **-ve**, or (placed after the second word like -**que**). **sepulc(h)rum, -ī** (*n*), tomb, grave.
2 **Calvus**: a close friend of Catullus (see Catullus 53), whose wife, Quintilia, has died.
3 **quō dēsīderiō**: ablative of means. **dēsīderium, -ī** (*n*), desire, longing (for a lost person or thing).
4 **ōlim**, once, of old. **mittō, mittere** (3), **mīsī, missum**, to give up, let go. Possibly, **missās** = **āmissās**, from **āmittō, āmittere** (3), **āmīsī, āmissum**, to lose.
5 **nōn tantō . . . dolōrī . . . est Quīntiliae** (6): double dative, "(it) is not a matter of such great grief to Quintilia. . . ." "(it) does not cause as much grief for Quintilia. . . ."
 mors: i.e., Quintilia's. **immātūrus, -a, -um**, premature, untimely.
6 **quantum . . . tuō**: = **quantum (Quīntilia) gaudet (in) amōre tuō**.

. . . mūtīs . . . sepulcrīs. . . .

44

CATULLUS 96

To Calvus, on the Sad Occasion of His Wife's Death

Catullus tries to console Calvus with the thought that death may not be a final break between the living and the dead.

1   Sī quicquam mūtīs grātum acceptumve sepulcrīs
2   accidere ā nostrō, Calve, dolōre potest,
3   quō dēsīderiō veterēs renovāmus amōrēs
4   atque ōlim missās flēmus amīcitiās,
5   certē nōn tantō mors immātūra dolōrī est
6   Quīntiliae, quantum gaudet amōre tuō.

1. What general proposition is Catullus stating in lines 1–4? How does he apply this to the specific situation in lines 5–6?

2. What kind of relationship does this poem suggest exists between the living and the dead?

3. Which beat, dactyl or spondee, predominates in this poem? With what effect? What is metrically unusual about lines 1 and 5?

4. How do the sentiments of this poem compare to those in the following passage in a letter from Sulpicius to Cicero on the death of Tullia, Cicero's beloved daughter?

Nūllus dolor est, quem nōn longinquitās temporis minuat ac molliat. Hoc tē exspectāre tempus, ac nōn eī reī sapientiā tuā tē occurrere, tibi turpe est. Quod sī quis etiam īnferīs sēnsus est, quī illīus in tē amor fuit pietāsque in omnēs suōs, hoc certē illa tē facere nōn vult.

(Epistulae ad familiares, IV.5.6)

There is no grief that the passage of time does not lessen and soothe. For you to extend this time rather than to use your wisdom to take care of the grief is shameful of you. But if any consciousness belongs to the inhabitants of the underworld, such was your daughter's love for you and devotion to her family that certainly this is not what she wants you to do.

METER: elegiac couplet (see Catullus 70).

1 **aequor, aequoris** (*n*), sea.

2 **ad** (+ *acc.*), at, for the purpose of. *__īnferiae__, __-ārum__ (*f pl*), offerings for the dead, funeral rites. Such offerings at the site of the grave might have included milk, honey, wine, and flowers.

3 **ut . . . mortis**: rephrase this as follows: **ut tibi postrēmum mūnus mortis dōnārem. postrēmus, -a, -um**, final, last. **dōnārem**: an imperfect subjunctive is used here and in line 4 instead of the present, as one would expect after **adveniō**, because the purpose of the author's trip originated in the past. *__mūnus, mūneris__ (*n*), duty, gift, tribute, offering.

4 **nēquīquam**, in vain. **alloquor, alloquī** (3), **allocūtus sum**, to address. **alloquerer**: imperfect subjunctive. **cinis, cineris** (*f*), ash.

5 **quandoquidem**, since, seeing that. **mihī**: dative of separation here and in line 6. **tētē**: a stronger form of **tē**.

6 **heu**, alas. **indignē**, undeservedly. Translate the adverb with **adēmpte**. **adimō, adimere** (3), **adēmī, adēmptum**, to carry off, take away. **adēmpte**: what case?

7 **intereā**, for the moment, for the time being, anyhow. **Haec** is the antecedent of **quae** and the object of **accipe** in line 9. A rearranging of the words in lines 7–9 may help your translation: **accipe haec, mānantia multum frāternō flētū, quae (in) prīscō mōre . . . īnferiās. prīscus, -a, -um**, ancient, old.

8 **trīstī mūnere**: "as a sad offering."

9 **multum** (*adv.*), much, abundantly. **mānō** (1), to drip, be wet. **flētus, -ūs** (*m*), crying, tears.

10 **in perpetuum**, forever, now and forever. **avē**: "hail!"

Adveniō hās miserās, frāter, ad īnferiās.

46

CATULLUS 101

Here rests his head upon the lap of Earth
A youth to Fortune and to Fame unknown.

(Thomas Gray, 1716–1771)

Catullus' brother has died in Asia Minor near Troy. How does Catullus
stress the distance he must go to the site of the grave? Why must he
travel there?

> Multās per gentēs et multa per aequora vectus
>   adveniō hās miserās, frāter, ad īnferiās,
> ut tē postrēmō dōnārem mūnere mortis
>   et mūtam nēquīquam alloquerer cinerem.
> 5 Quandoquidem fortūna mihī tētē abstulit ipsum,
>   heu miser indignē frāter adēmpte mihi,
> nunc tamen intereā haec, prīscō quae mōre parentum
>   trādita sunt trīstī mūnere ad īnferiās,
> accipe frāternō multum mānantia flētū,
> 10   atque in perpetuum, frāter, avē atque valē.

1. **What letters and sounds predominate in lines 1–4? Why? Read lines 1–4 aloud. How does Catullus use dactyls and spondees effectively here?**

2. **To whom is Catullus speaking in this poem? With that in mind, what particular kind of sadness is conveyed in line 4?**

3. **What feelings are expressed in lines 5–6? Look closely at the individual words in this couplet. What is the point behind using *tētē* and *ipsum* in combination? What is the force of the words *abstulit* and *adēmpte*? How do the three words *heu miser indignē* build on each other? Why is *mihi* repeated?**

4. **The words *nunc tamen intereā* in line 7 are difficult to translate. What turning point in the poem do they signify and with what earlier word does *tamen* correspond?**

5. **How many times do the words for brother and brotherly appear? Most ancient and modern epitaphs give full names and also single out qualities and accomplishments of the deceased. Do we learn anything about Catullus' brother? What, instead, is stressed?**

6. **Compare and contrast poem 101 with poem 96 on the death of Calvus' wife, Quintilia.**

7. **How well does Robert Fitzgerald translate this poem? Point out unusual and unexpected words and phrases in his version. Where has he taken the greatest liberties? How well do they succeed?**

> By strangers' coasts and waters, many days at sea,
>   I came here for the rites of your unworlding,
> Bringing for you, the dead, these last gifts of the living,
>   And my words—vain sounds for the man of dust.
>   Alas, my brother,
> You have been taken from me. You have been taken from me,
>   By cold Chance turned a shadow, and my pain.
>
> Here are the foods of the old ceremony, appointed
>   Long ago for the starvelings under earth:
> Take them; your brother's tears have made them wet; and take
>   Into eternity my hail and my farewell.

CATULLUS 109

More Promises

What does Lesbia promise Catullus in the opening lines of this poem?
What does Catullus hope will happen?

1   Iūcundum, mea vīta, mihi prōpōnis amōrem
2   hunc nostrum inter nōs perpetuumque fore.
3   Dī magnī, facite ut vērē prōmittere possit,
4   atque id sincērē dīcat et ex animō,
5   ut liceat nōbīs tōtā perdūcere vīta
6   aeternum hoc sānctae foedus amīcitiae.

METER: elegiac couplet (see Catullus 70).

1 **Iūcundum**: the first couplet may be translated in a variety of ways. One possibility is to take **iūcundum** and **perpetuum** (2) as predicate adjectives describing **amōrem** after the infinitive **fore**.
  prōpōnō, prōpōnere (3), **prōposuī, prōpositum**, to propose, proclaim, pledge.
  amōrem: translate with **hunc nostrum** (2) as "this love of ours."

2 **fore**: = **futūrum esse**. Give the principal parts of this verb. What tense is the infinitive?

3 **facite ut** (+ *subjunctive*), "make it that. . . ," "see to it that. . . ." The verb **facere** may be used to introduce a subjunctive clause, particularly in situations that imply effort. Point out the two subjunctives that are introduced by **facite ut**.
  prōmittō, prōmittere (3), **prōmīsī, prōmissum**, to promise.

5 **ut liceat**: is this a purpose clause or result clause? Try each. What is the difference in meaning and intent?
  tōtā . . . vītā: = **per tōtam vītam**.
  perdūcō, perdūcere (3), **perdūxī, perductum**, to draw out, extend.

6 **aeternus, -a, -um**, eternal, everlasting.

1. Why is *perpetuus amor*, as we understand *amor* from poem 5 and other poems of Catullus, a contradiction in terms?

2. What do we know, and what does Catullus hint at in lines 3–4 about the sincerity of Lesbia's promises? What is the point of using the three adverbial expressions, *vērē* (3), *sincērē* (4), and *ex animō* (4)? Can you distinguish among them?

3. What does Catullus mean in line 6 and how is it different from Lesbia's promises of *iūcundum . . . amōrem . . . perpetuumque* in lines 1–2? What political and historical associations might the words *sānctae foedus amīcitiae* have had for a Roman?

4. Point out an example of interlocked word order and of a transferred epithet in line 6. Why is each device effective here?

48

POEMS OF HORACE

Horace's Sabine farm

METER: second asclepiadean (the asclepiadean meters of Horace are based on a single pattern, the asclepiadean: $----\cup\cup-\|-\cup\cup-\cup\breve{}$). This poem alternates a glyconic ($---\cup\cup-\cup\breve{}$). In the first line of each couplet with an asclepiadean in the second line. A *diaeresis* (word-end after a metrical foot, here frequently coinciding with a pause in the sense of the line) occurs in the middle of the second line. Note the quantity of the initial *i* in **Iāpyga** (4) and **Īapetī** 7), and that in the word **Iovem** (40) the *i* is considered consonantal.

1 **Sīc**: Horace's friend Vergil is about to sail from Italy to Greece. The word **sīc** turns lines 1–4 into a promise: Horace will request good weather from the divinities (lines 1–4) if the ship (addressed in lines 5–8) transports Vergil safely to Greece. You may want to translate lines 5–8 first, then lines 1–4, as follows: **nāvis, quae dēbēs Vergilium crēditum tibi: reddās (Vergilium) incolumem fīnibus Atticīs, precor, et servēs dīmidium animae meae, sīc** ("for this," "in return") **dīva potēns Cyprī (regat) tē, sīc frātrēs Helenae (regant) tē, ventōrumque pater regat (tē), obstrictīs aliīs (ventīs) praeter Iāpyga**. **tē**: i.e., the **nāvis** (5). **dīva potēns Cyprī**: "the goddess who rules over Cyprus" (i.e., Venus, guardian of sailors, especially from her religious base on the island of Cyprus). **Dīva, frātrēs** (2), and **pater** (3) are all subjects of **regat** in line 3. Horace often uses a singular verb for more than one subject; **erat** in line 10 and **incubuit** in line 31 are two more examples.

2 **frātrēs Helenae**: i.e., Castor and Pollux. After their death, Castor and Pollux were immortalized as the two stars in the constellation Gemini. They became protectors of ships, especially during storms when flashes of light around the mast (St. Elmo's fire) indicated their presence. Castor, Pollux, Helen, and Clytemnestra were the offspring of Leda and Jupiter. **lūcidus, -a, -um**, bright, gleaming. **sīdus, sīderis** (*n*), star, constellation. **lūcida sīdera**: in apposition to **frātrēs Helenae**.

3 **ventōrum . . . pater**: i.e., Aeolus, king of the winds. **regō, regere** (3), **rēxī, rēctum**, to rule, (here) guide, look after. **regat**: what mood and construction?

4 **obstringō, obstringere** (3), **obstrīnxī, obstrīctum**, to bind up, tie up, confine. What form of the verb is **obstrictīs** and in what construction? **Iāpyx, Iāpygis** (*m*), the northwest wind. Winds are usually named after the place of their origin (the Iapyx originated in Iapygia, a Greek name for the southern heel of Italy, which also included Apulia) or from their geographical starting point (the west wind blows from west to east). In what direction does the Iapyx blow? Why is it not to be tied up? **Iāpyga**: Greek accusative singular.

5 **nāvis, quae . . . dēbēs** (6): "ship, you who owe. . . ." Vergil is a precious cargo or deposit that the ship must deliver safely. **crēdō, crēdere** (3), **crēdidī, crēditum** (+ *dat*.), to believe, entrust.

6 **Vergilius, -ī** (*m*), Publius Vergilius Maro (70–19 B.C.), author of the *Eclogues, Georgics,* and *Aeneid.* **fīnibus Atticīs**: = **ad fīnēs Atticōs.** **Atticus, -a, -um,** Attic (referring to a district in Greece that included Athens).

7 **reddō, reddere** (3), **reddidī, redditum**, to return, hand over, deliver. **reddās . . . servēs** (8): what mood, tense, and construction? **precor, precārī** (1), **precātus sum**, to pray.

8 **dīmidium, -ī** (*n*), half.

9 **Illī . . . erat** (10): dative of possession ("There was to that man. . . ." = "That man had. . . ."). Horace breaks from his address to the ship in order to talk about the first seafarer who sailed east on a course similiar to Vergil's. The demonstrative **illī** looks ahead to **quī** in line 10. **rōbur, rōboris** (*n*), oak. **triplex, triplicis**, three-fold, triple-plated.

10 **circā**: = **circum. pectus, pectoris** (*n*), chest, heart. **fragilis, -is, -e**, breakable, flimsy. **trux, trucis**, savage, fierce, rough.

11 **pelagus, -ī** (*n*), sea. **pelagō**: dative. *****ratis, ratis** (*f*), boat, craft.

12 **praeceps, praecipitis**, headlong, dangerous. *****Āfricus, -ī** (*m*), the southwest wind.

13 **dēcertō** (1), to fight. *****Aquilō, Aquilōnis** (*m*), the north wind. **Aquilōnibus**: = **cum Aquilōnibus.**

14 *****trīstis, -is, -e**, sad, dismal, gloomy. **trīstīs**: = **trīstēs**. In poetry you will often find this earlier accusative plural of *i*-stem nouns and adjectives. **Hyadēs, -um** (*f pl*), a group of seven stars in the constellation Taurus, associated with rainy days. **Hyadās**: accusative plural. **rabiēs, -ēī** (*f*), rage, frenzy. **Notus, -ī** (*m*), the south wind.

15 **quō nōn**: supply **est** and translate: "than which (i.e., the south wind) there is no. . . ." **arbiter, arbitrī** (*m*), judge, master, lord. *****Hadria, -ae** (*m*), Adriatic Sea, (east of Italy and vulnerable to a host of winds).

16 **tollere . . . freta**: translate in this order: (**seu Notus**) **tollere seu pōnere** (= **dēpōnere**) **freta vult**. **fretum, -ī** (*n*), strait, channel, (plural) sea.

50

HORACE I.3

For Vergil, on an Audacious Voyage

Following a prayer for Vergil's safe voyage to Greece, Horace explores the origin and existence of human daring and folly.

    Sīc tē dīva potēns Cyprī,
        sīc frātrēs Helenae, lūcida sīdera,
    ventōrumque regat pater
        obstrīctīs aliīs praeter Iāpyga,

5   nāvis, quae tibi crēditum
        dēbēs Vergilium: fīnibus Atticīs
    reddās incolumem, precor,
        et servēs animae dīmidium meae.

    Illī rōbur et aes triplex
10   circā pectus erat, quī fragilem trucī
    commīsit pelagō ratem
        prīmus, nec timuit praecipitem Āfricum

    dēcertantem Aquilōnibus
        nec trīstīs Hyadās nec rabiem Notī,
15   quō nōn arbiter Hadriae
        maior, tollere seu pōnere vult freta.

(continued)

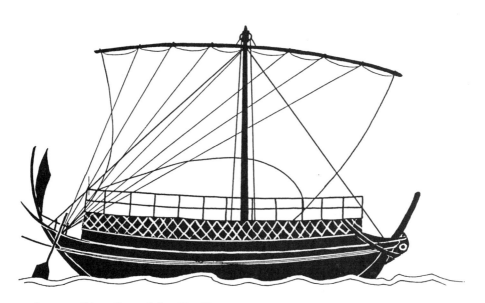

Nāvis, quae tibi crēditum dēbēs Vergilium.

17 **Quem**: interrogative adjective with **gradum**, object of **timuit**. The subject of **timuit** is still the first sailor who is described further in the next three lines.
   gradus, -ūs (m), step, approach.
18 **quī . . . natantia**: supply **vīdit**. **siccus, -a, -um**, dry. *mōnstrum, -ī (n)*, wonder, portent, monstrous creature. **natō (1)**, to swim, float. What do you think **mōnstra natantia** are?
19 **turbidus, -a, -um**, turbulent, stormy.
20 *īnfāmis, -is, -e*, ill-famed, notorious. **īnfāmīs**: = **īnfāmēs**. **scopulus, -ī (m)**, rock. **Ācroceraunia, -ōrum (n pl)**, a rocky promontory in the Ionian sea off the west coast of Greece and site of many shipwrecks.
21 **nēquīquam**, in vain. **abscindō, abscindere (3), abscidī, abscissum**, to separate, cut off. What is the object of this verb?
22 **prūdēns, prūdentis**, knowing, wise. **Ōceanō**: either an ablative of separation ("from . . ."), if Horace means that in the beginning land and ocean were mixed, or ablative of means ("by means of . . ."), if he means that originally all lands were connected. **dissociābilis, -is, -e**, unallied, incompatible, alien, intervening.
23 **impius, -a, -um**, unholy, disobedient, wicked.
24 **nōn tangenda**: neuter accusative plural, "not (intended) to be touched." **trānsiliō, trānsilīre (4), trānsiluī**, to leap across, skip over. **vadum, -ī (n)**, shallow water, (plural) sea.
25 **perpetior, perpetī (3), perpessus sum**, to endure. **Audāx . . . perpetī**: "daring to endure. . . ."
26 **ruō, ruere (3), ruī, rutum**, to rush, hasten. **vetō, vetāre (1), vetuī, vetitum**, to forbid, prohibit. *nefās (n, indeclinable)*, violation (of a divine command), crime, wrongdoing.
27 **Īapetī genus**: "offspring of Iapetus" (i.e., Prometheus). Iapetus was a Titan and father of Prometheus and Atlas, among others.
28 **fraus, fraudis (f)**, deceit, deception.
29 **Post ignem . . . subductum** (30), "After the removal of fire. . . ." Sometimes, as here, the participle expresses the main thought and is best translated as a noun. The most famous example of this is the phrase **ab urbe conditā**, which is normally translated, "from the foundation of the city." **aetherius, -a, -um**, heavenly. **aetheriā domō**: what case and why?
30 **maciēs, -ēī (f)**, poverty, famine, barrenness. **nova**: take with **cohors** (31). **febris, febris (f)**, fever.
31 **incumbō, incumbere (3), incubuī, incubitum** (+ *dat.*), to lie upon, fall upon. **cohors, cohortis (f)**, troop, battalion, host.
32 **sēmōtus, -a, -um**, remote, distant. **sēmōtī**: with **lētī** (33). What case? **prius**, formerly, previously. The adverb may be taken with either **sēmōtī** or **tarda**. **necessitās, necessitātis (f)**, necessity, inevitability, doom.
33 **lētum, -ī (n)**, death. **corripiō, corripere (3), corripuī, correptum**, to hasten, quicken.
34 **experior, experīrī (4), expertus sum**, to try, test. **Expertus**: supply **est**. **vacuus, -a, -um**, open, empty. **Daedalus, -ī (m)**, father of Icarus and inventor of wings for human flight. **āēr, āeris (m)**, air, sky. **āera**: Greek accusative singular.
35 **pinna, -ae (f)**, feather, wing. **pinnīs**: what case and why? **nōn . . . datīs**: = **negātīs**. For the use of *litotes*, see question 2 on Catullus 43.
36 **perrumpō, perrumpere (3), perrūpī, perruptum**, to force passage across, break through. **Acherōn, Acherontis (m)**, a river in the underworld. **Acheronta**: Greek accusative singular. **Herculeus, -a, -um**, Herculean, of Hercules. To which of the twelve labors is Horace alluding?
37 **Nīl . . . arduī est**: "There is no difficult situation. . . ." "Nothing is (too) difficult. . . ." **arduum, -ī (n)**, steep place, hardship, difficult situation. **arduī**: partitive genitive.
38 **stultitia, -ae (f)**, foolishness, folly.
39 *patior, patī (3), passus sum*, to suffer, allow, permit. The object of **patimur** is **Iovem** (40). *scelus, sceleris (n)*, crime, impiety.
40 **īrācundus, -a, -um**, angry, fuming. This is a good example of a *transferred epithet* (see the note on line 11 of Catullus 51). Which noun would you expect **īrācundus** to modify? Which noun does it modify? **Iovem**: from **Iuppiter, Iovis (m)**.
   pōnere: = **dēpōnere**. **fulmen, fulminis (n)**, bolt of lightning, thunderbolt.

Quem mortis timuit gradum,
   quī siccīs oculīs mōnstra natantia,
quī vīdit mare turbidum et
20   īnfāmīs scopulōs, Ācroceraunia?

Nēquīquam deus abscidit
   prūdēns Ōceanō dissociābilī
terrās, sī tamen impiae
   nōn tangenda ratēs trānsiliunt vada.

25 Audāx omnia perpetī
   gēns hūmāna ruit per vetitum nefās.
Audāx Īapetī genus
   ignem fraude malā gentibus intulit.

Post ignem aetheriā domō
30   subductum, maciēs et nova febrium
terrīs incubuit cohors,
   sēmōtīque prius tarda necessitās

lētī corripuit gradum.
   Expertus vacuum Daedalus āera
35   pinnīs nōn hominī datīs;
   perrūpit Acheronta Herculeus labor.

Nīl mortālibus arduī est;
   caelum ipsum petimus stultitiā, neque
per nostrum patimur scelus
40   īrācunda Iovem pōnere fulmina.

1. A traditional "send-off" poem (in Greek, *propemptikon*) generally included some or all of the following: grief and protest over the departure of a friend or loved one, prayers for a safe voyage and return, and a curse on the inventor of sailing. Which of these conventions has Horace used in I.3? Support your answer with reference to the text.

2. What indications are there in lines 1–8 that Horace and Vergil are close friends?

3. What is the specific setting of lines 9–20 and about whom is Horace talking? What attitude do you think Horace is taking toward this person? What are the literal and figurative meanings of the clause *Illī rōbur et aes triplex circā pectus erat* (9–10)? What is special about the word order in the clause *quī fragilem trucī commīsit pelagō ratem* (10–11)?

4. What conclusion does Horace draw in lines 21–24? What words in particular seem especially revealing? Why?

5. What mythological figures and events does Horace allude to in lines 25–36 and what do they have in common?

6. Compare lines 37–40 to lines 21–24. Which statement on human audacity is stronger? In what way?

7. In seeking a fuller understanding of this poem, one must address two questions that are often raised: what relationship exists between the opening prayer for Vergil's safety and Horace's digression on human audacity, and does the poem actually condemn this human audacity?

8. The 1st person verb *patimur* (39), would include Horace himself in the charge leveled against enterprising individuals. Is human audacity to be condemned or accepted as part of the scheme of things? What evidence in this poem supports your answer?

METER: fourth asclepiadean. The pattern is:

(asclepiadean, two lines) — — — ⌣ ⌣ — ‖ — ⌣ ⌣ — ⌣ ⌣
(pherecratean) — — — ⌣ ⌣ — ⌣
(glyconic) — — — ⌣ ⌣ — ⌣ ⌣

1 **Quis**: = **quī**. Take the interrogative adjective with **gracilis . . . puer**. The boy is aggressively pursuing Pyrrha (= **tē** in line 1), about whom we will hear more as the poem unfolds. **multā . . . in rosā**: "amid many a rose," "on a bed of roses." **gracilis, -is, -e**, slender.

2 **perfundō, perfundere** (3), **perfūdī, perfūsum**, to soak, drench. **liquidus, -a, -um**, fluid, flowing. **urgeō, urgēre** (2), **ursī**, to press, woo, embrace. **odor, odōris** (*m*), smell, fragrance, perfume.

3 **Pyrrha, -ae** (*f*), the woman to whom the poem is addressed. In Greek, *Pyrrha* means "redhead," from the Greek word *pyr*, "fire." **antrum, -ī** (*n*), cave, grotto.

4 **Cui . . . ?**: "For whom . . . ?" *****flāvus, -a, -um**, yellow, golden-yellow. **religō** (1), to tie back. **coma, -ae** (*f*), hair.

5 **simplex munditiīs**: "simple in your refinements." **munditia, -ae** (*f*), refinement, elegance. **heu**, alas. **quotiēns**, how often, how many times. **fidem**: supply **mūtātam**. Pyrrha's faithfulness (**fidem**) and the support of the gods (**deōs**) will often seem mutable and unpredictable to the boy.

6 **flēbit**: the subject is **puer**. **asper, aspera, asperum**, rough, harsh. The words **aspera nigrīs aequora ventīs** (6–7) are a good example of *interlocked word order*. For the poetic device, see question 1 on Catullus 87.

7 *****aequor, aequoris** (*n*), sea. **aequora**: object of **ēmīrābitur** (8).

8 **ēmīror, ēmīrārī** (1), **ēmīrātus sum**, to wonder at, be astonished at. **īnsolēns, īnsolentis**, unaccustomed (i.e., to the sight), surprised, inexperienced.

9 **fruor, fruī** (3), **frūctus sum** (+ *abl.*), to enjoy, delight in, possess. **crēdulus, -a, -um**, trusting, gullible. **aureus, -a, -um**, golden, resplendent.

10 **quī . . . spērat** (11): supply **tē futūram esse** to fill out the indirect statement. **vacuus, -a, -um**, free, available. *****amābilis, -is, -e**, lovely, lovable.

11 **nescius, -a, -um** (+ *gen.*), unaware of, ignorant of. *****aura, -ae** (*f*), breeze.

12 **fallāx, fallācis**, false, deceitful, treacherous. **Miserī**: supply **sunt puerī**.

13 **intemptātus, -a, -um**, untried, untested. *****niteō, nitēre** (2), to shine, glitter. **Mē**: translate in this order: **sacer pariēs tabulā vōtīvā indicat mē suspendisse ūvida vestīmenta deō potentī maris. tabula, -ae** (*f*), tablet. Survivors of a shipwreck would set up a tablet and hang up "wet" clothes as a dedication to Neptune.

14 **vōtīvus, -a, -um**, votive, vowed, promised. **pariēs, parietis** (*m*), wall (here, of a shrine or temple). **indicō** (1), to show, proclaim. **ūvidus, -a, -um**, wet.

15 **suspendō, suspendere** (3), **suspendī, suspēnsum**, to hang up. **suspendisse**: why is an infinitive used here, and what tense is it? **potentī . . . deō** (16): dative or ablative? How does the context help you decide?

16 **vestīmentum, -ī** (*n*), clothing, garment.

What slender Youth bedew'd with liquid odours
Courts thee on Roses in some pleasant Cave,
    Pyrrha? for whom bind'st thou
    In wreaths thy golden Hair,

Plain in thy neatness? O, how oft shall he
On Faith and changed Gods complain, and Seas
    Rough with black winds and storms
    Unwonted shall admire,

Who now enjoys thee credulous, all Gold;
Who always vacant, always amiable
    Hopes thee; of flattering gales
    Unmindful. Hapless they

To whom thou untried seem'st fair. Me in my vow'd
Picture the sacred wall declares t'have hung
    My dank and dropping weeds
    To the stern God of Sea.

(John Milton)

HORACE 1.5

To Pyrrha

> Quis multā gracilis tē puer in rosā
> perfūsus liquidīs urget odōribus
>   grātō, Pyrrha, sub antrō?
>   Cui flāvam religās comam,

5   simplex munditiīs? Heu quotiēns fidem
> mūtātōsque deōs flēbit et aspera
>   nigrīs aequora ventīs
>   ēmīrābitur īnsolēns,

> quī nunc tē fruitur crēdulus aureā,
10   quī semper vacuam, semper amābilem
>   spērat, nescius aurae
>   fallācis. Miserī, quibus

> intemptāta nitēs. Mē tabulā sacer
> vōtīvā pariēs indicat ūvida
15   suspendisse potentī
>   vestīmenta maris deō.

1. **What is happening in the first stanza? How do the order and choice of words reflect the scene?**

2. **Why is the boy crying in the second stanza? What discovery has he made? Discuss Horace's use of winds and water to symbolize the boy's discovery.**

3. **Compare the word order in the phrase *tē fruitur crēdulus aureā* (9) to that in *gracilis tē puer* (1). What reversal has taken place? Comment on the effectiveness of repetition in lines 9–10.**

4. **What is a "false breeze" (*aurae fallācis*, 11–12) and why would it be dangerous to a sailor and a lover? What pun might Horace be making on the words *aurae fallācis*?**

5. **What *persōna* (for a definition, see question 2 on Catullus 8) does Horace adopt in the final stanza? Why are allusions to the sea so prominent in this poem? What do the poet and the boys have in common?**

6. **What do the words *flāvam* (4), *aureā* (9), *nitēs* (13), and the name Pyrrha tell us about Pyrrha's attraction to boys? Where else in the poem does Horace use color effectively?**

7. **Ronald Storr spent many years collecting translations of this poem. The result: *Ad Pyrrham, a Polyglot Collection of Translations* (Oxford, 1955) with 451 versions in twenty-six languages. One version from that collection is quoted on the opposite page. How well does it succeed?**

1 **Vidēs**: the subject is Thaliarchus, addressed in line 8, with whom Horace is sharing his thoughts on the proper enjoyment of youth. *****ut**, how. **altā . . . nive**: ablative of description ("with . . ."). Translate with **stet** or **candidum**. **stet**: what mood and construction? The subject is **Sōracte**. *****nix, nivis** (*f*), snow.
candidus, -a, -um, bright, gleaming.

2 **Sōracte, Sōractis** (*n*), Mt. Soracte, about 25 miles north of Rome. **nec iam**: "and (how) no longer." **sustineant**: the subject is **silvae** (3). **onus**: i.e., of snow. What declension, gender, and case?

3 **gelū, -ūs** (*n*), ice, cold.

4 **cōnstō, cōnstāre** (1), **cōnstitī, cōnstātum**, to stand still. **cōnstiterint**: what mood and tense? **acūtus, -a, -um**, sharp, piercing.

5 *****frīgus, frigoris** (*n*), cold, coldness, chill. **lignum, -ī** (*n*), wood, log. **ligna**: object of **repōnēns**. **super** (+ *abl.*), on, high upon. **focus, -ī** (*m*), hearth, fireplace.

6 **largē**, freely, abundantly. **repōnō, repōnere** (3), **reposuī, repositum**, to place, pile up. **benignus, -a, -um**, kind, generous, liberal. **benignius**: what degree of the adverb?

7 *****dēprōmō, dēprōmere** (3), **dēprōmpsī, dēprōmptum**, to bring out, fetch. **quadrīmus, -a, -um**, four-year-old. *****Sabīnus, -a, -um**, Sabine. The Sabine region of Italy, where Horace had his simple estate, was northeast of Rome. **Sabīnā . . . diōtā**: ablative of separation. Presumably, the wine, as well as the jar, is Sabine.

8 **Thaliarchus, -ī** (*m*), a fictitious young man whose name in Greek means "master of ceremonies." *****merum, -ī** (*n*), undiluted wine, wine.
diōta, -ae (*f*) (*Greek loan word, meaning* two-eared), jar.

9 **permittō, permittere** (3), **permīsī, permissum**, to surrender, leave. **dīvus, -ī** (*m*), god. **quī simul**: "for as soon as they (i.e., the gods). . . ." *****simul**: = **simul ac**, as soon as.

10 **sternō, sternere** (3), **strāvī, strātum**, to force down, calm, still. **strāvēre**: = **strāvērunt**. **aequore**: = **in aequore**. **fervidus, -a, -um**, hot, raging.

11 **dēproeliāns, dēproeliantis**, struggling, battling. **dēproeliantīs**: = **dēproeliantēs**. *****cupressus, -ī** (*f*), cypress tree. Note that the names of trees are feminine in the 2nd declension.

12 **agitō** (1), to toss, shake, stir. **ornus, -ī** (*f*), ash tree. The cypress and ash are taller than most trees and are proportionally more subject to the force of the winds.

13 **Quid . . . crās**: indirect question, with **quaerere**. **sit futūrum**: "is going to be," "is to happen." The word **futūrum** modifies **quid** and is an adjective here.
fuge: = **nōlī**, don't (+ infinitive).

14 **quem . . . dabit**: the clause is the object of **appōne**. **quem . . . cumque**: translate as one word with **diērum** dependent on it, "whatever (of) days." The separation of a compound word into its parts with other words in between is called *tmesis*.
Fors, Fortis (*f*), Fate. See pages 3–4 of the Introduction for a general account of Horace's philosophy. **lucrum, -ī** (*n*), profit, gain. **lucrō**: dative of purpose with **appōne**, "for profit," "as gain."

15 **appōnō, appōnere** (3), **apposuī, appositum**, to apply, reckon, count. *****dulcis, -is, -e**, sweet. **dulcīs**: = **dulcēs**. **amor, amōris** (*m*), love, pleasure of love.

16 **spernō, spernere** (3), **sprēvī, sprētum**, to reject, scorn. **puer**: "while a boy," "in youth." **chorēa, -ae** (*f*), dance. **tū chorēās**: what verb do you need to supply?

HORACE I.9

Horace on Enjoying One's Youth

In the first stanza of this poem Horace presents Thaliarchus with a vision of chill winter. What is Thaliarchus urged to do in the remainder of the poem?

> Vidēs ut altā stet nive candidum
> Sōracte, nec iam sustineant onus
>   silvae labōrantēs, gelūque
>   flūmina cōnstiterint acūtō.
>
> 5   Dissolve frīgus ligna super focō
> largē repōnēns atque benignius
>   dēprōme quadrīmum Sabīnā,
>   Ō Thaliarche, merum diōtā.
>
> Permitte dīvīs cētera, quī simul
> 10 strāvēre ventōs aequore fervidō
>   dēproeliantīs, nec cupressī
>   nec veterēs agitantur ornī.
>
> Quid sit futūrum crās, fuge quaerere et
> quem Fors diērum cumque dabit, lucrō
> 15   appōne nec dulcīs amōrēs
>   sperne puer neque tū chorēās,

(continued)

Mōns Sōracte

17 **dōnec . . . mōrōsa** (18): "as long as moody (**mōrōsa**) white-old-age (**cānitiēs**) is far away from you-in-your-bloom (**virentī**)." **vireō, virēre** (2), **viruī**, to be green with vegetation, be full of youthful vigor. **cānitiēs, -ēī** (*f*), white coloring, grayness, old age.

18 **mōrōsus, -a, -um**, set in one's ways, hard to please, moody. Although the root of this adjective is **mōs, mōris** (*m*), custom, Horace may well want us to hear in the background the similar-sounding word, **mors, mortis** (*f*), death. **Nunc**: the scene changes to a vision of springtime in Rome. **campus**: = **Campus Martius**, the large playing field outside the old walls of Rome. **Campus, āreae** (18), and **susurrī** (19) are all subjects of **repetantur** (20). **ārea, -ae** (*f*), open area, square.

19 **lēnis, -is, -e**, soft, gentle. **sub** (+ *acc.*), at the approach of, just before. **susurrus, -ī** (*m*), sigh, whisper.

20 **compositus, -a, -um**, established, appointed. **compositā . . . hōrā**: what case? Why? **repetantur**: what mood and construction?

21 **nunc . . . pertinācī** (24): supply the present subjunctive of the verb **repetere** for the two subjects, **rīsus** (22) and **pignus** (23). Word order: **et nunc grātus rīsus, prōditor latentis puellae, ab** (from) **intumō angulō** (**repetātur**) **pignusque, dēreptum lacertīs aut digitō male pertinācī,** (**repetātur**). *****lateō, latēre** (2), **latuī**, to be concealed, hide. **prōditor, prōditōris** (*m*), betrayer. **intumus, -a, -um**, inner, secret.

22 **rīsus, -ūs** (*m*), laughter. **angulus, -ī** (*m*), corner (i.e., hiding place).

23 **pignus, pignoris** (*n*), pledge. **pignus . . . pertinācī** (24): Horace is describing a simple and universal rite of youthful romance. A boy might try to take a bracelet from the girl's arm or a ring from her finger as a pledge (**pignus**) of her love. She will put up only a minimum of resistance. **dēripiō, dēripere** (3), **dēripuī, dēreptum**, to tear off, snatch away. **lacertus, -ī** (*m*), upper arm, arm. **lacertīs . . . digitō** (24): what case and why?

24 **digitus, -ī** (*m*), finger. **male** (*adv.*), badly, (here, idiomatic) scarcely, barely. **pertināx, pertinācis**, resisting.

dōnec virentī cānitiēs abest
mōrōsa. Nunc et campus et āreae
    lēnēsque sub noctem susurrī
        compositā repetantur hōrā,

20

nunc et latentis prōditor intumō
grātus puellae rīsus ab angulō
    pignusque dēreptum lacertīs
        aut digitō male pertinācī.

1. Look closely at Horace's description of Mt. Soracte, the trees, and the rivers in the first stanza. What correspondence do you find between them and aspects of human old age and death?
2. How does the second stanza contrast with the first? What is the role of fire and wine?
3. Cite three tenets of Horace's Epicurean worldview that are stated in lines 9–18. What words and images does Horace use to make them concrete?
4. The key to the transition from wintry Mt. Soracte and thoughts of impending old age and death to springtime and youthfulness in Rome may be found in the contrast between the words *virentī* and *cānitiēs* in line 17. What are the root meanings of *virēre* and *cānitiēs*? What does each word mean in terms of human attributes? How might these two words connect the opening and closing scenes?
5. What sounds predominate in stanza 1 and why? What do you notice about the placement of the words *Sōracte, silvae,* and *flūmina* in the first stanza and of the imperatives in stanzas 2, 3, and 4? Find an example of interlocked word order in the second stanza. For what reason(s) would Horace use a complex word order in the last stanza? How does it reflect the action?

: fifth asclediadean (a "greater" asclepiadean line that adds an extra choriamb ($-\cup\cup-$) to the regular line). The pattern is: $\_\_\_\cup\cup-\|-\cup\cup-\|-\cup\cup-\cup\overset{\smile}{-}$. Note that this longer line has two diaereses.

1 **Tū nē quaesieris**: "Please don't ask" (the perfect subjunctive with **nē** is a more personal way of making a negative command than **nōlī** with the infinitive). Horace is addressing Leuconoe (2). **nefās**: supply **est**. **quem . . . fīnem** (2): = **quem (fīnem) mihi, quem fīnem tibi. . . .**

2 *** dī**: = **deī** (nominative plural). **dederint**: what mood, tense, and construction? **Leuconoē, Leuconoēs** (*f*), the literal meaning of this name in Greek is "whiteminded." Other possible meanings in the context of this poem are "clear-minded" or "simpleminded." **nec**: = **et nē**. **Babylōnius, -a, -um**, Babylonian. **Babylōniōs . . . numerōs** (3): Babylonian astrologers were well known for their "numerical" calculations and predictions of the future.

3 **temptāris**: = **temptāveris**. Same use of the perfect subjunctive with **nē** as in line 1. **Ut melius**: "How much better" (+ infinitive). **quicquid erit**: object of **patī**. **quicquid**: neuter nominative singular, "whatever." **patior, patī** (3), **passus sum**, to endure, accept.

4 **tribuō, tribuere** (3), **tribuī, tribūtum**, to assign, allot. **ultimus, -a, -um**, final, last. **ultimam**: supply **hiemem**.

5 **quae**: what is the antecedent? What gender, number, and case is **quae**? **oppositīs . . . pūmicibus**: "upon the opposing pumice rocks." **dēbilitō** (1), to weaken, wear down. **pūmex, pūmicis** (*m*), pumice, a soft volcanic rock commonly used for smoothing surfaces (see the note to line 8 in Catullus 22). Pumice would be worn away more easily by the sea than another type of rock such as granite. Horace, possibly, is suggesting that the rocks, in addition to the sea, are being worn down.

6 **Tyrrhēnus, -a, -um**, Tyrrhenian (name of the sea west of Italy, also called the Etruscan or Tuscan Sea). **sapiō, sapere** (3), **sapīvī**, to be sensible, be wise. In what mood are **sapiās, liquēs**, and **resecēs** in lines 6–7? Why? **liquō** (1), to remove sediment from, strain. **spatium, -ī** (*n*), space, length (of time). **spatiō brevī**: "with space (allotted for our hopes) being short," "with the length of time (for our lives) being short."

7 **resecō** (1), to cut back, prune. **invidus, -a, -um**, envious, jealous, greedy.

8 ***aetās, aetātis** (f), age, (here) time. **carpō, carpere** (3), **carpsī, carptum**, to pluck, seize, grasp, enjoy. **quam minimum**: "as little as possible." **crēdulus, -a, -um** (+ *dat.*), trusting in. **posterum, -ī** (*n*), the future, time to come, next day.

HORACE 1.11

Carpe Diem.

The following poem expresses a popular request in Western literature, that a young woman indulge in the present and not put enjoyment off to a future time. In lines 1–3, what is Horace urging Leuconoe not to do? What reason(s) would he have for telling her this?

1   Tū nē quaesieris, scīre nefās, quem mihi, quem tibi
2   fīnem dī dederint, Leuconoē, nec Babylōniōs
3   temptāris numerōs. Ut melius, quicquid erit, patī,
4   seu plūrēs hiemēs, seu tribuit Iuppiter ultimam,
5   quae nunc oppositīs dēbilitat pūmicibus mare
6   Tyrrhēnum. Sapiās, vīna liquēs, et spatiō brevī
7   spem longam resecēs. Dum loquimur, fūgerit invida
8   aetās: carpe diem, quam minimum crēdula posterō.

1. **What do the words *hiemēs* and *ultimam* in line 4 stand for in terms of human life? What effect does the winter have on the sea? What could the sea symbolize in this situation? Try to explain the strange inversion that Horace makes, that the sea does not wear down the rocks but instead is worn down against the rocks.**

2. **What advice does Horace give to Leuconoe in lines 6–7? Specifically, what activity is meant by the words *vīna liquēs* (6)? The original meaning of the verb *sapere* is "to taste," and the verb *resecāre* means "to cut back." How do these two words reinforce the message contained in the phrase *vīna liquēs*?**

3. **Why is time called *invida* in line 7? What tense is *fūgerit* and why is this choice of tense significant?**

4. **The root meaning of the verb *carpere* is "to pluck." Why is it a good choice of words for the pithy and famous expression, *carpe diem*?**

5. **Read the poem in meter. Is it slow or fast? Why does the beat work well with the message of the poem?**

6. **Compare and contrast Horace's entreaty to Leuconoe here with Catullus' plea to Lesbia in poem 5. Which poem is more direct? How do you account for your answer?**

7. **Read the following well-known poem by Robert Herrick (1591–1674). To whom is it addressed? What is requested of them? How is that request different from those contained in Horace I.11 and Catullus 5? Where else, especially in the use of words and images that suggest the passage of time, is this poem different from those of Horace and Catullus?**

To the Virgins, to Make Much of Time

Gather ye rosebuds while ye may:
  Old Time is still a-flying;
And this same flower that smiles today,
  Tomorrow will be dying.

The glorious lamp of heaven, the sun,
  The higher he's a-getting,
The sooner will his race be run,
  And nearer he's to setting.

That age is best which is the first,
  When youth and blood are warmer;
But being spent, the worse, and worst
  Times, still succeed the former.

Then be not coy, but use your time;
  And while ye may, go marry:
For, having lost but once your prime,
  You may for ever tarry.

METER: fourth asclepiadean (see Horace I.5).

1 **nāvis**: Horace is addressing a ship and expressing serious concerns about its situation and condition. Most commentators from ancient times to now have treated this poem as an *allegory* (see question 2 for a definition of this term). Since the state was occasionally compared to a ship in the ancient world, the ship in this poem has often been discussed as the ship of state. Recent critics, however, citing the presence of vocabulary from love poetry in the last stanza and alert to other words that have a human reference (e.g., **genus** and **nōmen** in line 13) suggest that on one level, at least, the ship may be a woman whom Horace is warning.
referent: what mood and tense? Who or what is the subject?

2 ***flūctus**, **-ūs** (*m*), wave. **occupō** (1), to get possession of, seize.

3 **ut**: what meaning of **ut** do you expect after **vidēs**? Cf. line 1 of Horace I.9.

4 **nūdum . . . Āfricō** (5): supply the present subjunctive of **sum** and use the following order: latus (sit) nūdum rēmigiō et mālus (sit) saucius celerī Āfricō. **nūdum rēmigiō**: "stripped of oars." **latus**, **lateris** (*n*), side (of the human body or of any other object).

5 **mālus**, **-ī** (*m*), mast. **saucius**, **-a**, **-um**, wounded.

6 **antemna**, **-ae** (*f*), yardarm (i.e., the wooden arm of a mast that holds the sail in place). **gemō**, **gemere** (3), **gemuī**, **gemitum**, to groan, creak. **fūnis**, **fūnis** (*m*), rope, cable (which was tied around the hull to prevent the wood from being displaced).

7 **dūrō** (1), to endure, withstand. **carīna**, **-ae** (*f*), keel, hull, (plural) ship. The figure of speech in which a part represents the whole is called *synecdoche*. **Carīnae** for **nāvis** is an example of this device. Find another in this poem.

8 **possint**: introduced by **ut** in line 3. **imperiōsus**, **-a**, **-um**, commanding, overwhelming. **imperiōsius**: what degree of the adjective? Identify number, gender, and case.

9 **tibi**: dative of possession. **integer**, **integra**, **integrum**, whole, intact. **linteum**, **-ī** (*n*), sail.

10 **nōn dī**: "nor (are) your gods (intact)." Apparently there has been damage to the ship's figurehead, where images of gods were painted. **iterum pressa . . . malō**: translate together. **Pressa** modifies the subject of the verb **vocēs**. **iterum**, again. **vocēs**: potential subjunctive, "you might call upon." **malō**: "by misfortune," "by danger."

11 **quamvīs** (+ *subjunctive*), although, however much. **Ponticus**, **-a**, **-um**, Pontic (referring to the Pontus, an area south of the Black Sea, noted for good timber). **pīnus**, **-ī** (*f*), pine. Take **pīnus** and **fīlia** (12) in apposition to the subject of the verb **iactēs** (13), "however much you, a . . . (and) a . . . , boast. . . ."

12 **nōbilis**: genitive, modifying **silvae**.

13 **iactō** (1), to show off, boast. **inūtilis**, **-is**, **-e**, useless, unavailing, ineffective. The adjective modifies both **genus** and **nōmen**.

14 **nīl**: = **nōn** (with **fīdit**). **pingō**, **pingere** (3), **pīnxī**, **pictum**, to paint, decorate. Ancient ships were often decorated with bright colors and designs. **nāvita**, **-ae** (*m*): = **nauta**, **-ae** (*m*). **puppis**, **puppis** (*f*), stern (of a ship), (plural) ship.

15 **fīdō**, **fīdere** (3), **fīsus sum** (+ *dat.*), to put trust in, believe in. **nisi . . . lūdibrium** (16): "unless you owe sport (**lūdibrium**) to the winds," "unless you are to be a plaything of the winds" (and have no control over the future). **caveō**, **cavēre** (2), **cāvī**, **cautum**, to beware.

17 **Nūper**: translate lines 17–20 in this order, (Tū, nāvis,) quae (erās) nūper sollicitum taedium mihi, (sed quae es) nunc dēsīderium . . . , vītēs. . . .
nūper, recently, not long ago. **sollicitus**, **-a**, **-um**, worrisome, troublesome. **taedium**, **-ī** (*n*), source of boredom, source of weariness, annoyance.

18 **dēsīderium**, **-ī** (*n*), desire, object of longing. **nōn levis**: = **gravis**. What rhetorical device is this?

19 **interfūsus**, **-a**, **-um**, poured amid, spread throughout. **interfūsa**: here, with an accusative object, **nitentīs . . . Cycladās** (20).

20 **vītēs**: from what verb? What mood and construction? **Cyclades**, **Cycladum** (*f pl*), a group of islands in the Aegean whose "shining" shores must have attracted ships in spite of storms and difficult landings. **Cycladās**: Greek accusative plural.

HORACE I.14

The Beauty of the Ship

> When, staunchly entering port,
> After long ventures, hauling up, worn and old,
> Batter'd by sea and wind, torn by many a fight,
> With the original sails all gone, replaced, or mended,
> I only saw, at last, the beauty of the Ship.
> (Walt Whitman, 1819-1897)

Ō nāvis, referent in mare tē novī
flūctūs! Ō quid agis? Fortiter occupā
   portum! Nōnne vidēs, ut
     nūdum rēmigiō latus

5 et mālus celerī saucius Āfricō
antemnaeque gemant, ac sine fūnibus
   vix dūrāre carīnae
     possint imperiōsius

aequor? Nōn tibi sunt integra lintea,
10 nōn dī, quōs iterum pressa vocēs malō.
   Quamvīs Pontica pīnus,
     silvae fīlia nōbilis,

iactēs et genus et nōmen inūtile,
nīl pictīs timidus nāvita puppibus
15   fīdit. Tū, nisi ventīs
     dēbēs lūdibrium, cavē.

Nūper sollicitum quae mihi taedium,
nunc dēsīderium cūraque nōn levis,
   interfūsa nitentīs
20   vītēs aequora Cȳcladās.

1. **Describe the condition of the ship according to lines 1–10. What does Horace fear in lines 11–16? Look closely at Horace's choice of adjectives in lines 1–16. Which ones are particularly vivid? How well do they succeed in conveying the wretched condition of the ship? Why would it be "useless" for the ship to boast of its origin (13)?**

2. **In the final stanza Horace tells us that his attitude toward the ship has recently changed. Most ancient and modern critics agree that the strong expression of the poet's feeling for the ship and the use of such personal words as *dēsīderium* and *cūra* are indications that we should read the poem as an *allegory* (a work in which the action and characters are understood both literally and as referring in a one-to-one correspondence to something else, usually historical, moral, or philosophical in nature; the most famous example being John Bunyan's *Pilgrim's Progress*). In the generation after Horace, the scholar Quintilian identified the elements of the poem as follows: *nāvem prō rē pūblicā, flūctūs et tempestātēs prō bellīs cīvīlibus, portum prō pāce atque concordiā*. According to Quintilian, how are we to understand the boat, the stormy waves, and the port?**

3. **If we accept Quintilian's interpretation of the poem, what might account for Horace's change of heart and sudden worry about the ship? Discuss the meaning of lines 19–20 in light of the quotation from Quintilian.**

METER: sapphic (see Catullus 51).

1 **Integer . . . eget** (2): the subject, an imaginary person, is understood. Translate: "A man, blameless in . . . and free from . . . , does not need. . . ." **integer, integra, integrum**, faultless, blameless in (+ genitive). **pūrus, -a, -um**, free from (+ genitive).

2 **egeō, egēre** (2), **eguī** (+ *abl.*), to need. The ablatives **iaculīs, arcū**, and **pharetrā** (4) depend on this verb. **Maurus, -a, -um**, Moorish, African. **iaculum, -ī** (*n*), javelin. **arcus, -ūs** (*m*), bow.

3 **venēnātus, -a, -um**, poisoned, poison-tipped. **gravidus, -a, -um**, heavy, filled with (+ ablative).

4 **Fuscus, -ī** (*m*), Aristius Fuscus, a close friend of Horace. **pharetra, -ae** (*f*), quiver (a holder of arrows).

5 **Syrtis, Syrtis** (*f*), a dangerous sandbank off the coast of Libya, (plural) African deserts. **Syrtīs**: = **Syrtēs**. **iter**: what gender and case? **aestuōsus, -a, -um**, hot, burning.

6 **factūrus**: supply **est**. The subject is the same as in the first stanza. What form and tense is **factūrus**? **inhospitālis, -is, -e**, inhospitable, unfriendly.

7 **Caucasus, -ī** (*m*), a mountain range east of the Black Sea. **quae loca**: = **loca quae**. **loca**: the second object of the preposition **per** (6). **fābulōsus, -a, -um**, fabled, storied.

8 **lambō, lambere** (3), **lambī**, to lap, splash. **Hydaspēs, Hydaspis** (*m*), a tributary of the Indus River.

9 **namque**, for, for once. **mē**: the object of **fūgit** (12); modified by **inermem** (12). **lupus, -ī** (*m*) wolf. Subject of **fūgit** (12).

10 **cantō** (1), to sing. Present tense verbs in **dum** clauses are often translated into English as imperfects. *****Lalagē, Lalagēs** (*f*), the name of Horace's real or imaginary girlfriend, which in Greek means "babbler" or "prattler." Here, take **meam . . . Lalagēn** as direct object of **cantō**, as if it were the name of a tune. **Lalagēn**: Greek accusative singular. **ultrā** (+ *acc.*), beyond.

11 **terminus, -ī** (*m*), boundary, boundary mark. **vagor, vagārī** (1), **vagātus sum**, to wander. **expediō, expedīre** (4), **expedīvī, expedītum**, to put aside, dismiss. **expedītīs**: what form, tense, and construction?

12 **inermis, -is, -e**, unarmed, defenseless.

13 **quālis, -is, -e**, such a. **portentum, -ī** (*n*), portent, monster. Here, object of **alit** in line 14 and of **generat** in line 15. **mīlitāris, -is, -e**, military, warring.

14 **Daunias, Dauniadis** (*f*), the land of Daunus. Daunias is another name for Apulia, known for its fighting prowess and oak forests, and once ruled by the legendary king Daunus. **alō, alere** (3), **aluī, altum**, to nourish, raise. **aesculētum, -ī** (*n*), oak forest. **lātīs . . . aesculētīs**: ablative of place where ("in . . .").

15 **Iuba, -ae** (*m*), Juba (the name of a North African king). *****tellūs, tellūris** (*f*), land. **generō** (1), to produce, give birth to. *****leō, leōnis** (*m*), lion.

16 **āridus, -a, -um**, dry, barren. **nūtrīx, nūtrīcis** (*f*), nurse (of an infant), wet nurse. **ārida nūtrīx**: an *oxymoron* (see note on line 1 of Catullus 46). Take in apposition to **Iubae tellūs**.

17 **Pōne . . . campīs**: word order: **Pōne mē** (in) **pigrīs campīs ubi**. . . . **piger, pigra, pigrum**, unfertile, inactive.

18 **aestīvus, -a, -um**, summer. **recreō** (1), to revive, bring to life again.

19 **quod latus mundī**: = **latus mundī quod**. This phrase is loosely parallel to **ubi** in line 17. **quod**: object of **urget** (20). **latus, lateris** (*n*), side, corner, region. **mundus, -ī** (*m*), world. **nebula, -ae** (*f*), cloud. **nebulae . . . Iuppiter** (20): subjects of **urget** (20).

20 **Iuppiter**: an example of *metonymy*, the use of a word that evokes something else (here, stormy weather) through close association without actually naming it. **urgeō, urgēre** (2), **ursī**, to press, oppress.

21 **pōne**: supply **mē** (cf. line 17). **sub . . . sōlis** (22): in mythology, the four-horse chariot of the sun was driven across the sky by Helius or Sol; its lowest point would have been midway, near the Tropics. **currus, -ūs** (*m*), chariot. *****nimium** (*adv.*), exceedingly, very. **propinquus, -a, -um**, neighboring, near, close.

22 **negātā**: "denied," "barred" (+ dative).

23 **dulce**: = **dulciter**.

HORACE I.22

A True Lover Need Fear No Danger.

What are the conditions under which a man can travel without weapons to the dangerous sites listed in the second stanza? Why will he be safe?

Integer vītae scelerisque pūrus
nōn eget Maurīs iaculīs neque arcū
nec venēnātīs gravidā sagittīs,
    Fusce, pharetrā,

5   sīve per Syrtīs iter aestuōsās
sīve factūrus per inhospitālem
Caucasum vel quae loca fābulōsus
    lambit Hydaspēs.

Namque mē silvā lupus in Sabīnā,
10   dum meam cantō Lalagēn et ultrā
terminum cūrīs vagor expedītīs,
    fūgit inermem;

quāle portentum neque mīlitāris
Daunias lātīs alit aesculētīs
15   nec Iubae tellūs generat, leōnum
    ārida nūtrīx.

Pōne mē pigrīs ubi nūlla campīs
arbor aestīvā recreātur aurā,
quod latus mundī nebulae malusque
20   Iuppiter urget;

pōne sub currū nimium propinquī
sōlis in terrā domibus negātā:
dulce rīdentem Lalagēn amābō,
    dulce loquentem.

1.   What pattern do you see in the geographical direction and physical setting of the locations mentioned in the second stanza?

2.   What is the connection between the imaginary person in stanzas 1 and 2 and Horace in stanza 3? What unusual event has happened to Horace? Why was he safe?

3.   What clues are there in stanzas 3 and 4 that show Horace is being playful?

4.   How would you characterize the regions of the world listed in the last two stanzas? If Horace had continued his line of thought from the opening stanza, what conclusion would you have expected him to make in lines 23–24? How does he surprise us? What has happened to the moral seriousness with which we began the poem?

5.   Lines 23–24 echo line 5 in Catullus 51 and include a reference to speaking from Sappho's original (see Catullus 51 for a translation), which Catullus had left out. Why does Horace mimic Catullus? With the Greek meaning of Lalage's name in mind, account for Horace's inclusion of the phrase *dulce loquentem*.

6.   Find examples of interlocked word order, suspenseful word order, and *asyndeton* (omission of a conjunction or conjunctions where they would be expected). Explain the use of *chiasmus* (see question 1 on Catullus 84) in line 1. Read the final two lines aloud. What letters and sounds are stressed?

METER: fourth asclepiadean (see Horace I.5). In line 4, **silvae** is pronounced **siluae** and scanned as three syllables.

1 **Vītās**: from what verb? **īnuleus, -ī** (*m*), fawn. The dative depends on **similis**, which modifies **Chloē**. **Chloē, Chloēs** (*f*), the young woman to whom the poem is addressed. In Greek, her name means "twig" or "green shoot."

2 **quaerentī**: what tense of the participle? With what does it agree? **pavidus, -a, -um**, frightened, scared. **montibus**: ablative of place where. **āvius, -a, -um**, roadless, pathless.

3 **nōn sine**: litotes: = **cum**. **vānus, -a, -um**, empty, groundless.

5 **mōbilis, -is, -e**, shaking, stirring, fluttering. **mōbilibus . . . foliīs** (6): "on the. . . ." *ver, vēris (n)*, spring. **vēris**: the genitive depends on **adventus** (6). **inhorrēscō, inhorrēscere** (3), **inhorruī**, to shiver, begin to rustle. For *inceptive* verbs, see the note on line 3 of Catullus 46.

6 **adventus, -ūs** (*m*), arrival. **folium, -ī** (*n*), leaf. **viridis, -is, -e**, green. **rubus, -ī** (*m*), bramble, bush.

7 **dīmoveō, dīmovēre** (2), **dīmōvī, dīmōtum**, to push aside, move. **dīmōvēre**: = **dīmōvērunt**. **lacerta, -ae** (*f*), lizard.

8 **cor, cordis** (*n*), heart. Translate: **et (in) corde et (in) genibus**. **genū, -ūs** (*n*), knee. **tremō, tremere** (3), **tremuī**, to tremble. **tremit**: the subject is the fawn.

9 **atquī**, and yet. **tigris, tigris** (*f*), tiger. Word order: **ut aspera tigris**. **ut**, like, as. **asper, aspera, asperum**, rough, fierce, wild.

10 **Gaetūlus, -a, -um**, Gaetulian, North African. **-ve**, or (placed after the second word like **-que**). **frangere persequor**: = **persequor ut frangam**. An infinitive of purpose may be used in poetry. **persequor, persequī** (3), **persecūtus sum**, to follow, pursue, chase after.

11 **dēsinō, dēsinere** (3), **dēsiī, dēsitum** (+ *infinitive*), to stop, cease.

12 **tempestīva . . . virō**: in apposition to the subject of **dēsine** (11), "you, who are ready for a man. . . ." Explain the meaning of **tempestīvus** ("ripe," "mature," "ready") according to its root. **sequī**: from what verb? What form and tense?

HORACE I.23

Chloe's Difficult Rite of Passage

Horace sometimes uses the world of nature to represent aspects of the human life cycle. In this poem, Horace addresses Chloe, a young woman who has come of age, and he compares her to a fawn.

Vītās īnuleō mē similis, Chloē,
quaerentī pavidam montibus āviīs
    mātrem nōn sine vānō
        aurārum et silvae metū.

5 Nam seu mōbilibus vēris inhorruit
adventus foliīs, seu viridēs rubum
    dīmōvēre lacertae,
        et corde et genibus tremit.

Atquī nōn ego tē tigris ut aspera
10 Gaetūlusve leō frangere persequor:
    tandem dēsine mātrem
        tempestīva sequī virō.

1. **What frightens the fawn in the first stanza? What would these fears be in human terms if they were to apply to Chloe? Why is the fawn's mother frightened? Why would Chloe's mother be frightened?**

2. **What time of year is it? Describe the two movements of nature in stanza 2 that coincide with the new season. Why do they frighten the fawn? There is much movement and trembling in this stanza. Which words vividly evoke it?**

3. **From what two animals does Horace distinguish himself in the last stanza? Why? What is his final wish for Chloe?**

4. **The verb *frangere* in line 10 is an unusual word to use in this context, unless you know the meaning of Chloe's name. Explain.**

5. **Compare Chloe to Leuconoe in Horace I.11. Although Horace is trying to persuade the two women to focus on the present, how do the concerns and obsessions of each differ?**

6. **Compare this poem to Horace I.5 on Pyrrha. How might Horace explain to Chloe that his relationship to her was different from the one between Pyrrha and the *puer*? In particular, look closely at lines 1 and 9 in each poem and show how Horace has demonstrated the difference through clever use of word order.**

METER: alcaic (see Horace I.9). The word **antehāc** in line 5 is pronounced and scanned as two syllables, equivalent to ant(eh)āc.

1 *bibō, bibere (3), bibī, to drink. est bibendum: an impersonal use of the passive periphrastic; translate: "there must be. . . ." The defeat of Antony and Cleopatra at the battle of Actium in 31 B.C. and their subsequent deaths in Alexandria were the occasion for great celebration in Rome.

2 pulsō (1), to strike. pulsanda: supply est. Saliāris, -is, -e, Salian (referring to priests known for grand banquets), priestly. Take with dapibus in line 4.

3 ōrnō (1), to furnish, provide. pulvīnar, pulvīnāris (n), couch. Horace is referring to the lectisternium, an ancient ceremony of prayer or thanksgiving during which images of gods were placed on couches and served banquets.

4 tempus erat: a shift in tense to express a less urgent demand, "(it) would be the right time" (+ infinitive). daps, dapis (f), feast, banquet. sodālis, sodālis (m/f), comrade, friend.

5 antehāc, previously, before. nefās: supply erat.
   Caecubum, -ī (n), Caecuban wine. This was an expensive wine from Latium.

6 cella, -ae (f), cellar, storeroom. avītus, -a, -um, ancestral. Capitōlium, -ī (n), the Capitol. The two peaks of the Capitoline Hill were the Arx on the northern side, where, according to legend, the sacred geese of Juno warned the Romans of a night raid by the Gauls in 387 B.C., and the Capitol to the south. On the Capitol was Rome's most sacred temple, dedicated to Jupiter Optimus Maximus, Juno, and Minerva. It was here that consuls took their vows of office and generals concluded their triumphal processions with an offering of thanks. Capitōliō: dative of reference ("for . . .") to be translated after ruīnās, as imperiō is to be translated after fūnus in line 8.

7 rēgīna: i.e., Cleopatra. dēmēns, dēmentis, mad, insane. dēmentīs: modifying ruīnās even though it should logically go with rēgīna. What poetic device is this? dēmentīs: = dēmentēs.

8 fūnus, fūneris (n), funeral, death, destruction. fūnus et: = et fūnus.
   imperium, -ī (n), rule, empire.

9 contāminātus, -a, -um, unclean, filthy, tainted. contāminātō: with grege. *grex, gregis (m), flock, herd, gang. turpis, -is, -e, filthy, foul. turpium . . . virōrum: i.e., the perverted (according to the Romans) men of Cleopatra's court, which would have included eunuchs.

10 morbus, -ī (m), disease. morbō: ablative with turpium. quidlibet, anything at all. Object of spērāre. impotēns, impotentis, unable to stop, mad, crazy. The infinitive spērāre depends on this adjective.

12 ēbrius, -a, -um, drunk. minuō, minuere (3), minuī, minūtum, to make smaller, lessen, diminish. The subject is nāvis (13). furor, furōris (m), rage, madness. furōrem: i.e., of Cleopatra.

13 vix: take with ūna. sōspes, sōspitis, safe, saved.

14 lymphātus, -a, -um, maddened, crazed. mentem . . . lymphātam: i.e., again, of Cleopatra. Mareōticum, -ī (n), Mareotic wine (from the region of Lake Mareotis, near Alexandria in Egypt).

15 redigō, redigere (3), redēgī, redāctum, to bring back, force.

16 Caesar: i.e., Octavian, subject of redēgit (15), adurgēns (17), and daret (20).
   ab Ītaliā: an exaggeration for effect; the battle of Actium was fought off the coast of western Greece. volantem: supply rēgīnam.

17 rēmus, -ī (m), oar. adurgeō, adurgēre (2), to press toward, closely pursue. accipiter . . . vēnātor (19): translate in this order: velut accipiter (adurget) mollīs columbās aut citus vēnātor leporem. . . . accipiter, accipitris (m), hawk. velut, just as, as.

18 mollis, -is, -e, soft, gentle. mollīs: what number, gender, and case? columba, -ae (f), dove. lepus, leporis (m), hare. *citus, -a, -um, swift, quick.

19 vēnātor, vēnātōris (m), hunter. nivālis, -is, -e, snowy.

20 Haemonia, -ae (f), an old name for Thessaly in northern Greece. catēna, -ae (f), chain. catēnīs dare, to put in chains.

21 fātālis, -is, -e, deadly, destructive. Quae: "But she." generōsus, -a, -um, noble. generōsius: what does the ending indicate?

22 muliebriter, in a womanly way, like a woman.

23 expavēscō, expavēscere (3), expāvī, to fear greatly, dread. ēnsis, ēnsis (m), sword. latentīs . . . ōrās (24): "hidden shores," "safe haven."

24 reparō (1), to obtain again, seek instead.

68

HORACE I.37

Cleopatra's Triumph in Defeat

This is a complex poem on the defeat of Cleopatra at the battle of Actium in 31 B.C. and her subsequent suicide. In a concentrated poetic fashion, Horace looks at the quest for power and its consequence through the figures of Cleopatra and Octavian. What words vividly portray Cleopatra and her lust for power in the first sixteen lines? How does the portrayal of her change in the second half of the poem?

Nunc est bibendum, nunc pede līberō
pulsanda tellūs, nunc Saliāribus
    ōrnāre pulvīnar deōrum
        tempus erat dapibus, sodālēs.

5   Antehāc nefās dēprōmere Caecubum
cellīs avītīs, dum Capitōliō
    rēgīna dēmentīs ruīnās,
        fūnus et imperiō parābat

contāminātō cum grege turpium
10   morbō virōrum, quidlibet impotēns
    spērāre fortūnāque dulcī
        ēbria. Sed minuit furōrem

vix ūna sōspes nāvis ab ignibus,
mentemque lymphātam Mareōticō
15   redēgit in vērōs timōrēs
        Caesar, ab Ītaliā volantem

rēmīs adurgēns, accipiter velut
mollīs columbās aut leporem citus
    vēnātor in campīs nivālis
20   Haemoniae, daret ut catēnīs

fātāle mōnstrum. Quae generōsius
perīre quaerēns nec muliebriter
    expāvit ēnsem nec latentīs
        classe citā reparāvit ōrās.

(continued)

25 **Ausa**: "Having dared to," "Enduring to" (+ infinitive), from the semideponent verb
audēre. Lines 25–32 present a compressed view of Cleopatra's final moments.
There are a variety of ways to construe this passage. For instance, you will notice
that there are only participles in this passage; some commentators, therefore,
translate **ausa** as **ausa est**. **et**, even. **iaceō, iacēre** (2), **iacuī**, to lie (here, in
ruin). **vīsō, vīsere** (3), **vīsī, vīsum**, to look upon, gaze at. **rēgia, -ae** (*f*), palace,
royal city, capital.
26 **voltus, -ūs** (*m*), face, expression, countenance. **fortis et . . . trāctāre** (27): "and brave
(enough) to handle. . . ." **asper, aspera, asperum**, harsh, rough, scaly.
27 *****āter, ātra, ātrum**, black, deadly.
28 **combibō, combibere** (3), **combibī**, to drink in deeply. **corpore combiberet**: an unusual
choice of words. What is the traditional account of Cleopatra's suicide? Does
Horace allude to that here? **venēnum, -ī** (*n*), poison.
29 **dēlīberō** (1), to resolve. **dēlīberātā morte**: "in her resolution to die," "in having
chosen the manner of her death." **ferōx, ferōcis**, fierce, courageous, brave.
30 **saevus, -a, -um**, savage, cruel. **Liburna, -ae** (*f*), Liburnian galley (a small ship that
Octavian used to great advantage against Cleopatra at the battle of Actium).
saevīs Liburnīs: dative with **invidēns**. *****scīlicet**, certainly, clearly. **invideō,
invidēre** (2), **invīdī, invīsum** (+ *dat.*), to envy, begrudge, deny.
31 **prīvāta**: "as a private person" (i.e., no longer queen). **dēdūcī**: present passive infinitive depending on **invidēns**, "that she be led away." *****superbus, -a, -um**, magnificent, proud, haughty.
32 **humilis, -is, -e**, humble, submissive. **nōn humilis**: with **mulier**. **triumphus, -ī** (*m*),
triumph, triumphal procession, victory parade. **triumphō**: "in . . ." or "for . . ."

*. . . fortis et asperās trāctāre
serpentēs. . . .*

25 Ausa et iacentem vīsere rēgiam
voltū serēnō, fortis et asperās
tractāre serpentēs, ut ātrum
corpore combiberet venēnum,

dēlīberātā morte ferōcior;
30 saevīs Liburnīs scīlicet invidēns
prīvāta dēdūcī superbō
nōn humilis mulier triumphō.

1. **Rome is in a festive mood. What rhetorical device and grammatical construction emphasize the need for celebration in the first stanza? What is meant by the phrase *pede līberō*?**

2. **For a Roman, the word *rēx* recalled the Etruscan kings and foreign domination. What particular response would the carefully juxtaposed words *Capitōliō rēgīna* (6–7) have evoked?**

3. **The turning point of the poem is in the simile in lines 17–19. What transformation takes place? Who is now the intended victim? Who is the aggressor? What uncertainty do we now feel about the Roman celebration?**

4. **In the remainder of the poem Cleopatra grows in dignity and strength; she, in fact, becomes more Roman and even stoic. Where is this evident? Cite Latin words to support your answer.**

5. **One important theme of the poem is drinking, drunkenness, and sobriety. Find examples of Cleopatra's drunkenness. When does she sober up to reality? What is the irony of her final drink?**

6. **There are many poetic devices in this poem. Find examples of *anaphora* (see question 3 on Catullus 5), interlocked word order, *simile* and *metaphor* (see question 6 on Catullus 76), *alliteration* and *assonance* (see question 3 on Catullus 5), synecdoche, and litotes. It has been said that the art of poetry depends partly on the correct use of the letter *s*. Where does Horace succeed at that in this poem?**

7. **Consult a good history of Rome for an account of the battle of Actium and Cleopatra's suicide. Where has Horace taken considerable license in his presentation of the events? Also, compare Horace's account of the battle of Actium to the pictorial description of it on the divinely made shield of Aeneas in the following translation of lines 675–713 of Vergil's *Aeneid*, Book VIII. What are the major differences between each poet's approach to this historical event?**

The queen in the center called up her columns by sounding the tambourine of her land; she had as yet no thought of the pair of asps which fate held in store for her. Her gods, monstrous shapes of every species, even to the barking Anubis, leveled weapons against Neptune, Venus, and Minerva herself. In the battle's midst raged Mars, moulded in iron, and from the sky scowling Furies let loose their savagery; Strife with her robe rent strode in joy, and Bellona followed with her blood-stained scourge. But Apollo of Actium saw; and high on his vantage-point he already bent his bow. In dread of it, every Egyptian, the Indians, every Arab, and all the host of Sheba were on point of turning in flight. The queen herself could be seen calling on the winds and setting sail, pictured at the very moment when she shook the sail-sheets loose. The God whose Might is Fire [Vulcan] had portrayed her amid the massacre, pale with the pallor of impending death, as she sped over the waves before a north-west gale. Before her the River Nile, with sorrow expressed throughout his great length, opened his full robe, and with all his raiment invited the vanquished to the bosom of his blue waters and the refuge of his streams.

(translated by W. F. Jackson Knight)

METER: sapphic (see Catullus 51).

1 **Persicus**, **-a**, **-um**, Persian, eastern, exotic. **ōdī**, **ōdisse** (*perfect in form; present in meaning*), to hate, despise. **apparātus**, **-ūs** (*m*), luxurious preparation, pomp, display, parade.

2 **displiceō**, **displicēre** (2), **displicuī**, **displicitum** (+ *dat.*), to displease, be not pleasing. **displicent**: supply **mihi**. The subject is **corōnae**. **nectō**, **nectere** (3), **nexuī**, **nexum**, to bind, stitch, weave. **philyra**, **-ae** (*f*), bark (from the linden tree, especially well-suited for binding elaborate wreaths). **corōna**, **-ae** (*f*), garland, wreath, crown.

3 **mitte**: = **nōlī**, don't (+ infinitive). **sector**, **sectārī** (1), **sectātus sum**, to search, seek. **rosa**: the subject of **morētur**. **quō locōrum**: "in which spots," "places in which."

4 **sērus**, **-a**, **-um**, late, final, late-blooming. **morētur**: from **moror** (1). What mood, tense, and construction?

5 **simplex**, **simplicis**, plain, simple. ***myrtus**, **-ī** (*f*), myrtle (a common evergreen plant). **Simplicī . . . cūrō** (6): rephrase and translate: **cūrō ut adlabōrēs nihil simplicī myrtō**, "I am anxious that you (i.e., the **puer**). . . .," equivalent to **cūrō nē quid adlabōrēs** in classical Latin prose. **adlabōrō** (1), to work at, add.

6 **sēdulus**, **-a**, **-um**, fussy, diligent. This may modify the subject of **adlabōrēs** or **cūrō**. Which do you prefer and why? **minister**, **ministrī** (*m*), servant. In apposition to **tē**.

7 **dēdecet** (+ *acc.*), (it) is unsuitable for. Explain how **neque . . . dēdecet** (6–7) is an example of litotes. **artus**, **-a**, **-um**, thick, dense.
vītis, **vītis** (*f*), grape, vine.

Horace Extols the Simple Myrtle.

The first book of Odes *ends on a quiet, personal note, in strong contrast to the public spectacle in the previous poem on Cleopatra. Why is the last word of the poem a fitting close to the first book?*

1   Persicōs ōdī, puer, apparātūs,
2   displicent nexae philyrā corōnae:
3   mitte sectārī, rosa quō locōrum
4   sēra morētur.

5   Simplicī myrtō nihil adlabōrēs
6   sēdulus cūrō: neque tē ministrum
7   dēdecet myrtus neque mē sub artā
8   vīte bibentem.

1. What is the connection between the first two lines of the poem denouncing grand displays and the second two lines on not seeking a late-blooming rose?

2. What is Horace's advice to the young man in the second stanza? Which words stand in contrast to words in the first stanza? Which stanza makes a stronger impression on you? Why?

3. Several approaches to this poem are possible. As a companion piece to Horace I.37 on Cleopatra, it returns us to the private world of the poet, who in the end seems to prefer simple wine in the company of a young companion to the public celebration of the previous poem. Does this interpretation fit with your understanding of Horace's *persōna* as presented in earlier poems? See, especially, poem I.9 to Thaliarchus.

4. We are also presented with a poet who scorns "Eastern" productions (*Persicōs . . . apparātūs*), which in the terminology of poetry and rhetoric refer to flowery and excessive literary compositions. Instead, Horace prefers a simple crown of myrtle as his reward. Furthermore, a pun may be intended on the word *artā* (7), which phonetically resembles the word for art, *ars, artis (f)*, and suggests something that is tightly woven and compact, such as the poems of Horace. Do you agree with this interpretation? Why or why not?

5. If we take this poem as an invitation to a young man who, like Thaliarchus in poem I.9, is misguided on how to spend his youth, another set of meanings emerges. What might be distracting the young man, according to Horace? What can Horace offer him in its place? Two more puns may be detected in the words *morētur* (4) and *vīte* (8) due to their closeness in sound to the words *moriētur* and *vīta*. Explain the intent of these puns in the context of Horace's advice to the young man.

METER: alcaic (see Horace I.9). The last syllable of line 27 elides with the first syllable of line 28.

1 **aequus**, **-a**, **-um**, even, level. **mementō** (*imperative*), remember to (+ infinitive). **arduus**, **-a**, **-um**, difficult, trying.

2 **nōn secus**, not otherwise, and equally, just as. **in bonīs**: supply **rēbus**.

3 **īnsolēns**, **īnsolentis**, unusual, excessive. What word does **īnsolentī** modify? **temperātus**, **-a**, **-um**, restrained, unaffected. **temperātam**: parallel to **aequam** (1).

4 **laetitia**, **-ae** (*f*), joy, happiness. **moritūre Dellī**: "Dellius, soon to die," "Dellius, destined to die." Quintus Dellius, an acquaintance of Horace, was apparently an opportunist who at one time or another served under Cassius, Antony, and Octavian.

5 **maestus**, **-a**, **-um**, sad, mournful, unhappy. Sometimes, as here, a Latin adjective is better translated as an adverb. **vīxeris**: from what verb? What tense?

6 *grāmen, grāminis (*n*), grass.

7 **fēstus**, **-a**, **-um**, festive. **diēs fēstus**, public holiday. **reclīnō** (1), to recline, lean back. **reclīnātum**: "having reclined," "leaning back." **beō** (1), to make happy, enjoy. **beāris**: = **beāveris**.

8 **interiōre notā Falernī**: "with a choice brand of Falernian wine"; i.e., with a wine whose vintage label (**notā**) and storage in the rear (**interiōre**) of the wine shelf indicate a fine selection.

9 **quō**, for what purpose, to what end. **pīnus**, **-ī** (*f*), pine tree. **ingēns**, **ingentis**, huge, large. **albus**, **-a**, **-um**, white. **pōpulus**, **-ī** (*f*), poplar tree.

10 *umbra, **-ae** (*f*), shade. **hospitālis**, **-is**, **-e**, hospitable, friendly. **cōnsociō** (1), to unite in making, ally in extending. **amant**: "are accustomed to."

11 **rāmus**, **-ī** (*m*), branch. **quid**, why. **oblīquus**, **-a**, **-um**, sloping, slanting, winding.

12 *lympha, **-ae** (*f*), water. *fugāx, fugācis, fleeing, swift. **trepidō** (1), to rush hurriedly, scurry. **trepidāre**: with **labōrat**. *rīvus, **-ī** (*m*), stream.

13 **unguentum**, **-ī** (*n*), perfume. *brevis, **-is**, **-e**, short, short-lived. **brevīs**: = **brevēs**.

14 *flōs, flōris (*m*), flower, blossom. **amoenus**, **-a**, **-um**, lovely, pleasant. **ferre iubē**: supply **servōs** as the object of **iubē** and subject of **ferre**.

15 **sorōrum**: i.e., the Fates, who spin, measure, and cut the threads of our destinies.

16 **fīlum -ī** (*n*), thread. **trium**: from **trēs**. What case?

17 **Cēdēs**: i.e., at the time of death. **coemō, coemere** (3), **coēmī, coēmptum**, to buy up, acquire. **saltus, -ūs** (*m*), pasture land, rolling country.

18 **vīllā**: what is the difference between a **domus** and a **vīlla**? According to line 18, where is this **vīlla** located? **Tiberis, Tiberis** (*m*), Tiber River.
lavō, lavere (3), **lāvī, lautum**, to wash, splash.

19 **exstruō, exstruere** (3), **exstrūxī, exstrūctum**, to build up, pile up. **in altum**: "high."

20 **dīvitiae, -ārum** (*f pl*), riches, wealth. **dīvitiīs**: what case? Why? **potior, potīrī** (4), **potītus sum** (+ *abl.*), to get possession of, obtain, have control over.
*hērēs, hērēdis (*m/f*), heir.

21 **Dīvesne ... morēris** (23): word order: **nīl interest dīvesne** (et) **nātus ab Īnachō prīscō, an pauper et dē** (from) **īnfimā gente sub dīvō morēris**. *dīves, dīvitis, rich, wealthy. **-ne**: in an indirect question translate as "whether." **prīscus, -a, -um**, old, ancient. **nātus, -a, -um**, born, descended. **Īnachus, -ī** (*m*), a legendary king of ancient Argos in Greece.

22 **nīl interest**: "it makes no difference," "it does not matter." **pauper, pauperis**, poor. **īnfimus, -a, -um**, lowliest, most humble.

23 **sub dīvō morēris**: "you dwell under the open sky" (i.e., you are alive).

24 **victima**: "(seeing that you are) a victim." **nīl**: adverbial, "not," "not at all." **miseror, miserārī** (1), **miserātus sum**, to pity, have mercy. **miserantis**: what form and case? **Orcus, -ī** (*m*), another name for Pluto, king of the underworld.

25 **eōdem**, to the same place, for the same end. **omnium ... cumbae** (28): word order: **sors omnium** (in) **urnā versātur, exitūra sērius ōcius et impositūra nōs. ... omnium**: "of us all."

26 **versō** (1), to turn, shake. **urna, -ae** (*f*), urn, jar. **sērius ōcius**: "sooner or later."

27 **sors, sortis** (*f*), lot in life, fate. **exitūra**: translate the future participles **exitūra** and **impositūra** (28) by relative or independent clauses: "which (i.e., **sors**) will. . . ." or "and it will. . . ." **exeō, exīre** (*irreg.*), **exiī, exitum**, to go out, turn up.
aeternus, -a, -um, eternal, everlasting.

28 **exsilium, -ī** (*n*), exile, banishment. **cumba, -ae** (*f*), boat, craft (i.e., of Charon, the ferryman of the dead). Take **cumbae** as dative with **impositūra**, "on the craft," or as genitive with **exsilium**, "of the craft." In either translation the "craft" stands by metonymy for irreversible death.

74

HORACE II.3

Sooner or Later Charon's Boat Bears Us Away.

In the first half of this poem Horace urges Dellius both to accept modera-
tion and equanimity at all times and to adopt a **carpe diem** *attitude.*

Aequam mementō rēbus in arduīs
servāre mentem, nōn secus in bonīs
    ab īnsolentī temperātam
      laetitiā, moritūre Dellī,

5   seu maestus omnī tempore vīxeris,
seu tē in remōtō grāmine per diēs
    fēstōs reclīnātum beāris
      interiōre notā Falernī.

Quō pīnus ingēns albaque pōpulus
10 umbram hospitālem cōnsociāre amant
    rāmīs? Quid oblīquō labōrat
      lympha fugāx trepidāre rīvō?

Hūc vīna et unguenta et nimium brevīs
flōrēs amoenae ferre iubē rosae,
15   dum rēs et aetās et sorōrum
      fīla trium patiuntur ātra.

Cēdēs coēmptīs saltibus et domō
vīllāque, flāvus quam Tiberis lavit,
    cēdēs, et exstrūctīs in altum
20   dīvitiīs potiētur hērēs.

Dīvesne, prīscō nātus ab Īnachō,
nīl interest an pauper et īnfimā
    dē gente sub dīvō morēris,
      victima nīl miserantis Orcī.

25 Omnēs eōdem cōgimur, omnium
versātur urnā sērius ōcius
    sors exitūra et nōs in aeternum
      exsilium impositūra cumbae.

1. Describe the two scenes from nature in stanza 3. How are they different? How do they illustrate the two types of people in the previous stanza? What other reasons can you give for their presence in the poem? How might they anticipate the scene in the next two lines?

2. How do images of liquids and vegetation in lines 5–14 contribute to the *carpe diem* theme?

3. Lines 15–16 introduce a third theme, which was anticipated in Dellius' epithet, *moritūre*. What is this theme and how is it worked out in the second half of the poem? Do lines 1–14 or 15–28 leave a stronger impression? Why?

4. What is the role of the heir (20)?

5. Read lines 17–18 aloud. What consonants stand out in line 17? in line 18? How do they contrast and why?

6. Lines 21–28 are a good example of a Horatian thought that draws more strength from its expression than from its profundity. How does Horace use parallel phrasing, word placement, allusions, and repetition to achieve the intended effect?

1 **ēheu**, alas. **Postumus, -ī** (*m*), the person to whom this somber poem on the inevitability of death is addressed. Whether or not Horace had a particular person in mind, the name, from the root **post**, was often given to the last-born child or to a child born after the father's death.

2 **lābor, lābī** (3), **lāpsus sum**, to slide, slip by, fall away. ***pietās, pietātis** (*f*), dutifulness, devotion. Horace has chosen a very resonant word for his thoughts here. The Romans held the notion of **pietās** very close to their hearts, but as Horace reminds them, not even strict devotion to the gods, state, and family is enough to reverse the toll of time and the approach of death.

3 **rūga, -ae** (*f*), wrinkle. **rūgīs . . . senectae . . . mortī** (4): what case and why? **īnstāns, īnstantis**, pressing, urgent, persistent. **senecta, -ae** (*f*), old age.

4 **indomitus, -a, -um**, unrestrained, unconquerable.

5 **trecēnī, -ae, -a**, three hundred. **trecēnīs**: ablative of means, modifying **taurīs** (7). **quotquot eunt diēs**: "however many days go by," "each day of your life."

6 **plācō** (1), to soothe, appease, placate. **plācēs**: what mood and tense? What type of conditional sentence? **inlacrimābilis, -is, -e**, tearless, merciless.

7 **Plūtōna**: **Plūtōna, Gēryonēn** (8), and **Tityon** (8) are Greek accusatives. Pluto was the god of the underworld, Tityus was eternally damned for trying to rape Leto, and Geryon was a three-headed or triple-bodied king who was killed by Heracles. ***taurus, -ī** (*m*), bull. **ter amplum**: "triply large," "triple-bodied," "three-headed."

8 **trīstī**: what case? What word does it modify?

9 **compēscō, compēscere** (3), **compēscuī**, to confine, imprison. **undā . . . ēnāvigandā** (11): rephrase and translate as follows: **undā ēnāvigandā scīlicet omnibus, quīcumque. . . .**, "by water which certainly must be sailed across by all, everyone of us who. . . ." **unda, -ae** (*f*), wave, water (i.e., at the entrance to the underworld).

10 **quīcumque, quaecumque, quodcumque**, whoever, everyone who. **mūnus, mūneris** (*n*), gift, produce. **vēscor, vēscī** (3) (+ *abl*.), to eat, feed on.

11 **ēnāvigō** (1), to sail across, traverse. **rēgēs**: from **rēx, rēgis**.

12 **inops, inopis**, poor. **colōnus, -ī** (*m*), farmer.

13 **cruentus, -a, -um**, bloody. **Mārte . . . flūctibus**: identify case and usage. **Mārs, Mārtis** (*m*), Mars, war. **careō, carēre** (2), **caruī** (+ *abl*.), to be without, avoid.

14 **raucus, -a, -um**, hoarse, noisy, howling. Note that **Hadriae** is masculine.

15 ***autumnus, -ī** (*m*), autumn (generally an unhealthy time of year in Italy).

16 **metuō, metuere** (3), **metuī**, to fear. **Auster, Austrī** (*m*), the south wind.

17 **vīsō, vīsere** (3), **vīsī, vīsum**, to see, visit. **vīsendus**: supply **est**. The subjects of **vīsendus** are **Cōcȳtos** (18), **genus** (18), and **Sīsyphus** (20). **languidus, -a, -um**, sluggish. **flūmine languidō**: ablative of description or manner with **errāns** (18).

18 **Cōcȳtos, Cōcȳtī** (*m*), a river in the underworld. **Cōcȳtos**: Greek nominative singular. **errō** (1), to wander. **Danaus, -ī** (*m*), father of fifty daughters called the Danaïdes, forty-nine of whom killed their husbands on their wedding night and were punished in the underworld by having to fill leaky jars with water forever.

19 **damnō** (1) (+ *gen*.), to condemn to, punish with.

20 **Sīsyphus Aeolidēs**: "Sisyphus, son of Aeolus." Sisyphus, for various crimes, was sentenced to an eternity of pushing a rock up a hill and then watching it roll down.

21 **linquō, linquere** (3), **līquī**, to leave behind, abandon. **Linquenda**: supply **est**. What are the three subjects?

22 **neque . . . sequētur** (24): word order: **neque ūlla (arbor) hārum arborum, quās colis, sequētur tē, brevem dominum, praeter invīsās cupressōs. hārum**: from what pronoun? **colō, colere** (3), **coluī, cultum**, to cultivate, tend to.

23 **invīsus, -a, -um**, hated. The cypress tree was commonly associated with death, and cypress branches were often placed around the cremation site.

24 **dominus, -ī** (*m*), master, proprietor. **brevem dominum**: in apposition to **tē** (23).

25 **absūmō, absūmere** (3), **absūmpsī, absūmptum**, to consume, use up. **Caecuba . . . servāta** (26): neuter accusative plural, "Caecuban wine saved up," "bottles of Caecuban wine (presently) stored and locked." ***dignus, -a, -um**, worthy.

26 **centum**: with **clāvibus**. **clāvis, clāvis** (*f*), key. **merō . . . superbō** (27): ablative of means with **tinguet**.

27 **tinguō, tinguere** (3), **tīnxī, tīnctum**, to soak, splash, stain.

28 **pontificum potiōre cēnīs**: "better than (wines served at) the dinners of priests." Cf. lines 2–4 in Horace I.37 for another allusion to the sumptuous banquets of the high priests. ***pontifex, pontificis** (*m*), priest. **potior, potiōris**, better, superior.

76

HORACE II.14

The Inevitability of Death

How do the first two words of the following poem anticipate its theme?
What effect does Horace achieve by repeating the name Postumus in the
first line?

>   Ēheu fugācēs, Postume, Postume,
>   lābuntur annī, nec pietās moram
>   rūgīs et īnstantī senectae
>   adferet indomitaeque mortī;

5   nōn sī trecēnīs, quotquot eunt diēs,
>   amīce, plācēs inlacrimābilem
>   Plūtōna taurīs, quī ter amplum
>   Gēryonēn Tityonque trīstī

>   compēscit undā, scīlicet omnibus,
10   quīcumque terrae mūnere vēscimur,
>   ēnāvigandā, sīve rēgēs
>   sīve inopēs erimus colōnī.

>   Frūstrā cruentō Mārte carēbimus
>   frāctīsque raucī flūctibus Hadriae,
15   frūstrā per autumnōs nocentem
>   corporibus metuēmus Austrum:

>   vīsendus āter flūmine languidō
>   Cōcȳtos errāns et Danaī genus
>   īnfāme damnātusque longī
20   Sīsyphus Aeolidēs labōris.

>   Linquenda tellūs et domus et placēns
>   uxor, neque hārum, quās colis, arborum
>   tē praeter invīsās cupressōs
>   ūlla brevem dominum sequētur.

25   Absūmet hērēs Caecuba dignior
>   servāta centum clāvibus et merō
>   tinguet pavīmentum superbō
>   pontificum potiōre cēnīs.

1. **According to Horace, what is *pietās* incapable of doing (2–4)? Describe the stages of human life that Horace surveys here. How do conjunctions and the length of successive phrases bring attention to the three stages? Which stage receives the greatest emphasis?**
2. **Stanzas 2 and 3 expand on the notion of *pietās* and *indomita mors*. What is Horace saying in these lines and how does he make it vivid and concrete?**
3. **What tactics to avoid death does Horace survey in stanza 4? What conclusion does he draw in stanza 5?**

(continued)

PLUTO.

. . . nōn sī trecēnīs . . . plācēs inlacrimābilem Plūtōna taurīs. . . .

4. Lines 21–24 allude to the following passage (Book III, lines 894–911) in *De rerum natura* by the Epicurean poet Lucretius (ca. 94–ca. 55 B.C.). What is the point of comparison between Horace and Lucretius? Consider carefully the motive of each poet in discussing the inevitability of death. In what major way are the motives different?

"No longer now will your happy home give you welcome, no longer will your best of wives; no longer will your sweet children race to win the first kisses, and thrill your heart to its depths with sweetness. You will no longer be able to live in prosperity, and to protect your own. Poor man, poor man!" they say, "one fatal day has robbed you of all these prizes of life." But they do not go on to add: "No longer too does any craving possess you for these things." If they could see this clearly in mind and so conform their speech, they would free themselves from great anguish and fear of mind.

"Yes, you, as you now lie in death's quiet sleep, so you will be for all time that is to come, removed from all distressing pains; but we beside you, as you lay burnt to ashes on the horrible pyre, have bewailed you inconsolably, and that everlasting grief no time shall take from our hearts." Of such a speaker then we may well ask, if all ends in sleep and quiet rest, what bitterness there is in it so great that one could pine with everlasting sorrow.

(translated by W. H. D. Rouse and M. F. Smith)

5. Why does Horace call the heir "more worthy" in line 25? What sad truth does Horace convey by saying that the heir will stain the floor with the wine?

6. One measure of the power of this poem is the extent to which Horace negates most of the life-giving images of animals, liquids, and vegetation that we find in other poems. Look closely at these images in this poem and show how through context and use of adjectives Horace has reversed their life-enhancing attributes.

7. The buildup of details, the use of balanced phrasing, and the presence of evocative sounds also contribute to the forcefulness of the message. Where do you find carefully balanced lists of three phrases or nouns? What effect do the groupings by three have? The name Postumus is one example of a word that is repeated to accentuate the sad theme of this poem. What other word is repeated for the same effect? What sounds are stressed in lines 13–16? Explain why the three passive periphrastic constructions are very well suited for this poem.

8. With which lines of Horace's poem is the following most comparable?

Well, death don't have no mercy in this land.
I said, death don't have no mercy in this land.
Well, he'll come to your house and he won't stay long,
look around the room, one of your family will be gone.
Death don't have no mercy in this land.

(Reverend Gary Davis)

1 ***fōns, fontis** (*m*), fountain, spring. **Bandusia, -ae** (*f*), the name of a spring, possibly located near Horace's birthplace or his Sabine farm. A festival celebrating a spring was a common event in the countryside. The wreaths and wine were typical, but the sacrifice of a goat would have been an unlikely feature of the ceremony.
*splendidus, -a, -um, brilliant, lustrous, sparkling. **vitrum, -ī** (*n*), glass.

2 **dulcī . . . merō**: take these ablatives with **digne**, which is vocative and modifies **fōns**.

3 **dōnō** (1), to give as a present, offer, (passive) be presented with (+ ablative).
haedus, -ī (*m*), young goat, kid.

4 **cui**: dative of reference; here, translate as a genitive, "whose." **frōns, frontis** (*f*), forehead. **turgidus, -a, -um**, swollen. The ablative phrase **cornibus prīmīs** depends on **turgida** and suggests a young goat showing the first signs of a powerful life.

5 **venus, veneris** (*f*), love. **et venerem et proelia**: possibly *hendiadys* (see the note on line 2 of Catullus 12) = **proelia veneris**. **destinō** (1), to set one out for, mark one for (+ accusative).

6 **gelidus, -a, -um**, cool. **īnficiō, īnficere** (3), **īnfēcī, īnfectum**, to stain. The subject is **subolēs** in line 8.

7 **ruber, rubra, rubrum**, red. **sanguis, sanguinis** (*m*), blood.

8 **lascīvus, -a, -um**, playful, wanton, lusty. **subolēs, subolis** (*f*), offspring.

9 **Tē**: i.e., **fōns Bandusiae**. **flagrō** (1), to burn. **atrōx, atrōcis**, fierce, savage.
Canīcula, -ae (*f*), Dog Star (the brightest star in the sky, also called Sirius; it rose in July and indicated the beginning of the hot season).

10 **nesciō, nescīre** (4), **nescīvī**, not to know how (+ infinitive). **frīgus**: i.e., of drink or shade.

11 **fessus, -a, -um**, weary, tired. **vōmer, vōmeris** (*m*), plow. **vōmere**: what case and why?

12 **praebeō, praebēre** (2), **praebuī, praebitum**, to offer, provide. **pecus, pecoris** (*n*), cattle, herd. **vagus, -a, -um**, wandering.

13 **Fīēs**: "You will become one," "You will be counted among" (+ genitive). Horace promises the **fōns Bandusiae** that with this poem it will join the ranks of such famous Greek springs as Hippocrene, Arethusa, and Castalia.

14 **mē dīcente**: ablative absolute, almost setting a condition to the fame that will attend the spring, "upon my. . . ." "as long as I. . . ." The beautifully descriptive lines that follow capture the essence of the spring and the refreshing "gifts" it can offer. **dīcō, dīcere** (3), **dīxī, dictum**, to say, celebrate in words. **cavus, -a, -um**, hollow. **impositam**: supply **esse**. What tense and voice of the infinitive? Why is an infinitive used? **īlex, īlicis** (*f*), oak tree.

15 **saxīs**: ablative of place where or dative after the compound verb **impōnere**.
loquāx, loquācis, talkative, babbling.

16 **dēsiliō, dēsilīre** (4), **dēsiluī, dēsultum**, to leap down, tumble down.

Ō fōns Bandusiae. . . .

HORACE III.13

A Goat Is Sacrificed to the *Fōns Bandusiae*.

Horace elevates the **fōns Bandusiae**, *a relatively unknown local spring, to the ranks of other famous springs in ancient literature. From your reading of the poem, how would you characterize the* **fōns Bandusiae**? *What words describe it? How does the poet transform it into a metaphor?*

Ō fōns Bandusiae, splendidior vitrō,
dulcī digne merō nōn sine flōribus,
    crās dōnāberis haedō,
        cui frōns turgida cornibus

5   prīmīs et venerem et proelia destinat,
frūstrā: nam gelidōs īnficiet tibi
    rubrō sanguine rīvōs
        lascīvī subolēs gregis.

Tē flagrantis atrōx hōra Canīculae
10   nescit tangere, tū frīgus amābile
    fessīs vōmere taurīs
        praebēs et pecorī vagō.

Fīēs nōbilium tū quoque fontium,
mē dīcente cavīs impositam īlicem
15   saxīs, unde loquācēs
        lymphae dēsiliunt tuae.

1. **How is the goat characterized? What words describe it? What contrast do you see between the spring and the goat?**

2. **Steele Commager in *The Odes of Horace* has analyzed this poem as an extended metaphor for the artistic process. In such an interpretation, which figure, the spring or the goat, could be a metaphor for art and which one for life? Defend your answer with reference to the poem. Explain the sacrifice of the goat to the spring in this context. Also, how would you explain the two developments in stanza 3, that the elements do not affect the spring and that the spring offers refreshment to the tired bulls?**

3. **How else can you interpret the poem? Is it a meditation on life, with all its inexplicable conflicts and resolutions? On nature, where, possibly, balance is kept only through painful sacrifice? How would the details of the poem fit into these interpretations?**

4. **Poets before Horace paid tribute to such famous springs as Hippocrene and Arethusa for being the metaphorical source of inspiration from which they, as poets, could drink and find artistic expression for their great works. How is Horace's relation to the spring different according to the last stanza of this poem? Give possible reasons for the reversal of roles. How does the imagery in the last stanza bring the poem to a fitting close? What letters are emphasized?**

METER: first asclepiadean. The pattern is: $--- \smile\smile - \| - \smile\smile - \smile \underset{\smile}{-}$

1 **exigō, exigere** (3), **exēgī**, **exāctum**, to complete, construct, raise. **aere ... situ** (2): what case and why? **perennis, -is, -e**, lasting, durable. **perennius ... altius** (2): what degree of the adjective? Identify gender, number, and case.

2 **rēgālis, -is, -e**, royal. **situs, -ūs** (*m*), site, structure. **pȳramid, pȳramidis** (*f*), pyramid.

3 **quod**: what is the antecedent? What are the gender, number, and case of **quod**? **imber, imbris** (*m*), rain. **edāx, edācis**, consuming, greedy. **impotēns, impotentis**, raging, uncontrolled.

4 **possit**: a potential subjunctive, "(it) could." What are the four subjects of **possit**? **dīruō, dīruere** (3), **dīruī, dīrutum**, to tear apart, demolish, destroy.

5 **seriēs, -ēī** (*f*), series, succession.

6 **omnis**: "entirely," "altogether," "wholly." **multus, -a, -um**, much, great, considerable. **meī**: genitive of **ego**.

7 **Libitīna, -ae** (*f*), goddess of corpses and funerals. An example of metonymy; how? **usque**, continually, constantly. **posterus, -a, -um**, later, future.

8 **crēscō, crēscere** (3), **crēvī, crētum**, to grow. **laus, laudis** (*f*), praise. **laude**: with **recēns**. **recēns, recentis**, fresh. **Capitōlium, -ī** (*n*), Capitol, (by extension) Capitoline Hill. For the Capitol, see the note on line 6 of Horace I.37.

9 **scandō, scandere** (3), to climb, ascend. **tacitus, -a, -um**, quiet, silent.

10 **Dīcar ... modōs** (14): translate **Dīcar** with **prīnceps** (13) and **dēdūxisse** (14): "I will be talked about (i.e., famous), where . . . , for being the first (**prīnceps**) to have adapted (**dēdūxisse**). . . ." *****quā**, where.
violēns, violentis, forceful, raging. **obstrepō, obstrepere** (3), **obstrepuī**, to roar, resound.
Aufidus, -ī (*m*), a river in Apulia, the region of Horace's birth.

11 **pauper aquae**: "poor of (= in) water." Whom does **pauper** modify? How is this an example of a tranferred epithet? **Daunus, -ī** (*m*), an early king of Apulia.
agrestis, -is, -e, peasant, rural.

12 **rēgnō** (1) (+ gen., *a Greek construction*), to rule over. **ex humilī potēns**, "influential from a humble beginning." This phrase may fit best in your translation at the beginning of line 10.

13 **prīnceps, prīncipis**, first, foremost. By Horace's time the adjective **prīnceps**, a compound of the words **prīmus** and **capere**, had evolved into a noun with the meanings "chief," "leader," and "emperor." Although it will be difficult to keep the words **ex humilī potēns prīnceps** together in your translation, Horace expected his audience to be aware of the secondary meaning implied in the phrase —Horace has ascended from obscurity to become a powerful emperor (of poetry).
Aeolius, -a, -um, Aeolian, Aeolic (referring both to the name of the region in Greece, which included the island of Lesbos, home of the poets Sappho and Alcaeus, and to the name of the dialect that these two poets used).
carmen, carminis (*n*), song, poetry.

14 **dēdūcō, dēdūcere** (3), **dēdūxī, dēductum**, to lead away, bring, (of poetry) compose, adapt. **modus, -ī** (*m*), measure, meter. Horace claims to be the first to have brought Aeolic meters to Latin poetry. His extensive use of these meters in his poetry justifies his claim even though Catullus had used the Sapphic meter in two poems (Catullus 11 and 51). **Sūme**: what form? Who is the subject?
superbia, -ae (*f*), pride, proud honor, proud look.

15 **quaerō, quaerere** (3), **quaesīvī, quaesītum**, to seek, earn. **meritum, -ī** (*n*), merit, achievement (i.e., of his poetry). **Delphicus, -a, -um**, Delphic, of or belonging to Delphi (site of the oracle of Apollo, god of poets and the arts, for whom the laurel was sacred).

16 **laurus, -ī** (*f*), laurel. **cingō, cingere** (3), **cīnxī, cīnctum**, to wreathe, crown. **volēns, volentis**, willing, willingly. **Melpomenē, Melpomenēs** (*f*), one of the nine Muses, whose name derives from the Greek verb "to sing." **coma, -ae** (*f*), hair, head.

HORACE III.30

A Monument More Lasting Than Bronze

This poem, the final one in Book III, is a testament to the permanent worth of Horace's poetry. It employs the same meter as Horace I.1, the only two poems in the first three books of Odes *to do so, and together they are a frame around an impressive artistic achievement.*

Exēgī monumentum aere perennius
rēgālīque sitū pȳramidum altius,
quod nōn imber edāx, nōn Aquilō impotēns
possit dīruere aut innumerābilis

5   annōrum seriēs et fuga temporum.
Nōn omnis moriar multaque pars meī
vītābit Libitīnam: usque ego posterā
crēscam laude recēns, dum Capitōlium
scandet cum tacitā virgine pontifex.

10   Dīcar, quā violēns obstrepit Aufidus
et quā pauper aquae Daunus agrestium
rēgnāvit populōrum, ex humilī potēns
prīnceps Aeolium carmen ad Ītalōs
dēdūxisse modōs. Sūme superbiam

15   quaesītam meritīs et mihi Delphicā
laurō cinge volēns, Melpomenē, comam.

1. What claim does Horace make in lines 1–5? What concrete and abstract images does he use to do this?
2. With what aspect of Roman life does Horace link the survival of his poetry and endurance of his fame (6–9)? Why is it a fitting choice for Horace?
3. In lines 10–14, where does Horace expect to receive acclaim? Do you find this modest claim strange in the context of the poem? Why or why not? What features of his native land, Apulia, does he highlight by referring to Aufidus and Daunus? Exactly what is Horace proud of in these lines? Is it the excellence of his poetry?
4. Do you find his final request conceited? Self-congratulatory? Intentionally exaggerated? Are great poets equal to the fame they claim for themselves? Defend your answer with reference to this and other poems and poets you have read.
5. Find examples of metaphor, interlocked word order, litotes, parallel phrasing, and *hyperbole* (exaggeration). Explain the chiasmus in line 5. Since this is a poem in Horace's honor, note the strong placement of certain verbs and nouns at the beginning and end of lines. Which ones stand out?

Delphicā laurō cinge . . . comam.

METER: second archilochian (named after the Greek poet Archilochus). The first line of each couplet is dactylic hexameter (see Catullus 70), and the second line is a shortened version of the hexameter. The pattern is:

$$- \breve{\breve{\smile\smile}} \mid - \breve{\breve{\smile\smile}} \mid - \breve{\breve{\smile\smile}} \mid - \breve{\breve{\smile\smile}} \mid - \breve{\breve{\smile\smile}} \mid - \breve{\smile}$$

$$- \smile\smile \mid - \smile\smile \mid \stackrel{-}{\smile}$$

In line 17, the word **adiciant** is pronounced **adjiciant**, making the first syllable long, and in line 27, the *eu* in **Theseus** is a diphthong.

1 **diffugiō, diffugere** (3), **diffūgī**, to flee, disperse. **diffūgēre**: = **diffūgērunt**.
2 **coma, -ae** (*f*), hair, foliage, leaf. **comae**: nominative plural.
3 **mūtat ... vicēs**: "(it) undergoes changes." **dēcrēscō, dēcrēscere** (3), **dēcrēvī**, **dēcrētum**, to subside.
4 **praetereō, praeterīre** (*irreg.*), **praeteriī, praeteritum**, to pass by.
5 **Grātia, -ae** (*f*), a Grace. The three Graces were personifications of beauty. **geminus, -a, -um**, twin. **gemīnīsque sorōribus**: i.e., the other two Graces.
6 **nūdus, -a, -um**, naked, unclothed. **chorus, -ī** (*m*), a group of dancers.
7 **Immortālia ... diem** (8): word order: **annus et hōra, quae almum diem rapit, monet (tē) nē immortālia spērēs.** The object of this warning is Torquatus (23). **immortā-lia, -ōrum** (*n pl*), immortality. **almus, -a, -um**, nourishing, life-giving, bountiful.
9 **mītēscō, mītēscere** (3), to become mild, be softened. **Zephyrus, -ī** (*m*), Zephyr, the west wind. **prōterō, prōterere** (3), **prōtrīvī, prōtrītum**, to wear away, trample on.
10 **intereō, interīre** (*irreg.*), **interiī, interitum**, to die, perish. **simul**: = **simul ac**.
11 **pōmifer, pōmifera, pōmiferum**, fruit-bearing. **frūgēs, frūgum** (*f pl*), fruit, produce.
12 **brūma, -ae** (*f*), winter. **iners, inertis**, inactive, sluggish, lifeless.
13 **damnum, -ī** (*n*), loss. **reparō** (1), to repair, restore. Horace is alluding to the monthly cycle of the moon. **caelestis, -is, -e**, heavenly. **lūna, -ae** (*f*), moon.
14 **dēcidō, dēcidere** (3), **dēcidī**, to fall down, sink down, perish, die.
15 ***quō**, to which place, to where, where. **pius, -a, -um**, dutiful, devoted. **Aenēās ... Tullus ... Ancus**: Aeneas, the son of Anchises and Venus, was a Trojan hero, who, as recounted in Vergil's *Aeneid*, journeyed to Italy to found the Roman race; Tullus Hostilius and Ancus Marcius were the third and fourth kings of Rome.
16 **pulvis, pulveris** (*m*), dust.
17 **an**, whether. **adiciō, adicere** (3), **adiēcī, adiectum**, to throw on, add. **hodiernus, -a, -um**, today's, of today. **crāstinus, -a, -um**, tomorrow's, of tomorrow. **summa, -ae** (*f*), sum, total. Here, a dative.
18 **superus, -a, -um**, above, celestial.
19 **cūnctus, -a, -um**, all. **avidus, -a, -um**, greedy. **amīcō**: take with **animō** (20), "to your own self," "on your self."
20 **dederīs**: an idiomatic rendering of the verb **dare**, such as "to use" or "to spend," may work better in this context. Common sense and usage dictate that **dederīs** and **occiderīs** (21) are future perfect indicatives and not perfect subjunctives; the final *i* is long to fit the meter.
21 **semel**, once. **occidō, occidere** (3), **occidī, occāsum**, to fall, die. **Mīnōs, Mīnōis** (*m*), one of three judges in the underworld.
22 **arbitrium, -ī** (*n*), judgment, verdict.
23 **Torquātus, -ī** (*m*), a Roman about whom we know little. What can you deduce about him from lines 23–24? **fācundia, -ae** (*f*), eloquence.
24 **restituō, restituere** (3), **restituī, restitūtum**, to restore, bring back (to life).
25 **īnfernus, -a, -um**, lower, of the underworld. **tenebrae, -ārum** (*f pl*), darkness, shadows. **tenebrīs**: ablative of separation, with **līberat** (26).
Diāna, -ae (*f*), the virgin goddess whom Hippolytus, the son of Theseus, worshiped. After Hippolytus was killed, Diana tried hard to have him resurrected and, according to Horace (note the present tense of **līberat**), is still trying, unsuccessfully. **pudīcus, -a, -um**, chaste, virtuous.
27 **Lēthaeus, -a, -um**, of Lethe, of the underworld. **Thēseus, -ī** (*m*), slayer of the Mino-taur and king of Athens, who went with his friend Pirithous to kidnap Per-sephone from the underworld. They were tricked into sitting on a bench (some say the bench of Lethe or forgetfulness), to which they were chained. Hercules rescued Theseus but did not succeed in freeing Pirithous. Theseus, now dead and in the underworld, cannot free his friend, either. **cārus, -a, -um**, dear.
28 **vinculum, -ī** (*n*), chain. **Pīrithous, -ī** (*m*), Pirithous.

HORACE IV.7

". . . the most beautiful poem in ancient literature."

(A. E. Houseman, 1856–1936)

Horace celebrates the arrival of spring (1–6). Why does he introduce the Graces and the Nymphs? For us, what does the arrival of spring signify and how do we normally respond to the events described in the opening lines?

Diffūgēre nivēs, redeunt iam grāmina campīs
    arboribusque comae;
mūtat terra vicēs, et dēcrēscentia rīpās
    flūmina praetereunt;

5 Grātia cum Nymphīs geminīsque sorōribus audet
    dūcere nūda chorōs.
Immortālia nē spērēs, monet annus et almum
    quae rapit hōra diem.

Frīgora mītēscunt Zephyrīs, vēr prōterit aestās
10   interitūra, simul
pōmifer autumnus frūgēs effūderit, et mox
    brūma recurrit iners;
damna tamen celerēs reparant caelestia lūnae:
    nōs ubi dēcidimus,
15 quō pius Aenēās, quō Tullus dīves et Ancus,
    pulvis et umbra sumus.

Quis scit an adiciant hodiernae crāstina summae
    tempora dī superī?
Cūncta manūs avidās fugient hērēdis, amīcō
20   quae dederīs animō.

Cum semel occiderīs et dē tē splendida Mīnōs
    fēcerit arbitria,
nōn, Torquāte, genus, nōn tē fācundia, nōn tē
    restituet pietās;

25 īnfernīs neque enim tenebrīs Diāna pudīcum
    līberat Hippolytum,
nec Lēthaea valet Thēseus abrumpere cārō
    vincula Pīrithoō.

1. **What does Horace abruptly tell us in lines 7–8? How do his choice and arrangement of words make his point stronger?**
2. **How do lines 9–12 differ from lines 1–6? What seems to be the point here? Show how Horace has chosen his verbs for the seasons carefully and effectively. How is *brūma recurrit iners* (12) an oxymoron?**
3. **Lines 13–16 are the exact middle of the poem. What general truth does Horace present here? What allusions does he use to enlarge this comment on the human predicament?**
4. **What common Horatian themes are expressed concisely in lines 17–20? What device do you find in line 23 and why is it forceful here?**
5. **In the final lines we are far from the opening vision of springtime. Explain Horace's use of myth to generalize a point he made in lines 23–24.**

VOCABULARY

A

ā, ab (+ *abl.*), by, from, away from
abrumpō, -umpere (3), **-ūpī, -uptum**, to break off, break apart
absum, abesse (*irreg.*), **āfuī**, to be absent, be away, be far away
ac, and
accidō, -ere (3), **-ī**, to happen, result from
accipiō, -ipere (3), **-ēpī, -eptum**, to receive, get, take
ad (+ *acc.*), to, towards, at
admīror, -ārī (1), **-ātus sum**, to admire
adveniō, -venīre (4), **-vēnī, -ventum**, to arrive, come
*****aequor, -oris** (*n*), sea
aes, aeris (*n*), bronze
aestās, -ātis (*f*), summer
*****aetās, -ātis** (*f*), age, time
*****afferō, -rre** (*irreg.*), **attulī, allātum**, to bring
*****Āfricus, -ī** (*m*), southwest wind
ager, agrī (*m*), field, farming land
agō, agere (3), **ēgī, āctum**, to do
   grātiās agere, to give thanks
   vītam agere, to lead one's life
aliquī, aliqua, aliquid, some
aliquis, aliquid, someone, something, anyone, anything
alius, alia, aliud, other, another
alter, altera, alterum, a second, the next
altus, -a, -um, high, deep
*****amābilis, -is, -e**, lovely, lovable
*****amāns, amantis** (*m*), lover
amīca, -ae (*f*), girlfriend, mistress
amīcitia, -ae (*f*), friendship
amīcus, -ī (*m*), friend
amō (1), to love, like
*****amor, -ōris** (*m*), love
an, or
anima, -ae (*f*), soul
animus, -ī (*m*), soul, mind, heart
annus, -ī (*m*), year
aqua, -ae (*f*), water
*****Aquilō, -ōnis** (*m*), north wind
arbor, arboris (*f*), tree
*****artūs, -uum** (*m pl*), joints, limbs
*****aspiciō, -icere** (3), **-exī, -ectum**, to look at
at, but

*****āter, -tra, -trum**, black, deadly
atque, and
audāx, audācis, bold, daring, reckless
audeō, -dēre (2), **-sus sum** (+ *infinitive*), to dare
audiō (4), to hear, listen to
auferō, -rre (*irreg.*), **abstulī, ablātum**, to take away, wrench
*****aura, -ae** (*f*), breeze
*****auris, -is** (*f*), ear
*****autumnus, -ī** (*m*), autumn
aut, or
   aut . . . aut, either . . . or

B

*****bāsium, -ī** (*n*), kiss
*****beātus, -a, -um**, happy, prosperous
*****bellus, -a, -um**, pretty, nice, cute
bene, well
   *****bene velle** (+ *dat.*), to be fond of, like, respect
*****bibō, -ere** (3), **-ī**, to drink
bonus, -a, -um, good
*****brevis, -is, -e**, short, brief, short-lived

C

caelum, -ī (*n*), sky, heaven
Caesar, -aris (*m*), Caesar
campus, -ī (*m*), field, plain, playing field
*****candidus, -a, -um**, bright, dazzling, fair-skinned, striking
cēdō, -dere (3), **-ssī, -ssum**, to go away, depart
celer, -eris, -ere, swift
cēna, -ae (*f*), meal, dinner
*****cēnō** (1), to dine
centum, a hundred
certē, certainly, surely
cēterī, -ae, -a, the rest
circā (+ *acc.*), around
*****citus, -a, -um**, swift
classis, -is (*f*), fleet (of ships)
cōgitō (1), to think
cognōscō, -ōscere (3), **-ōvī, -itum**, to learn, (perfect) recognize, know

cōgō, -ere (3), **coēgī, coāctum,** to gather together, force
committō, -ittere (3), **-īsī, -issum,** to entrust
comparō (1), to compare
cornū, -ūs (*n*), horn (of an animal)
corpus, -oris (*n*), body
crās, tomorrow
crēdō, -ere (3), **-idī, -itum** (+ *dat.*), to believe, entrust
cum (+ *abl.*), with
cum, when, since
Cupīdō, -inis (*m*), Cupid, god of love
***cupressus, -ī** (*f*), cypress tree
cūr, why
cūra, -ae (*f*), care
cūrō (1), to care for, be anxious

D

dē (+ *abl.*), down from, from, about
dēbeō (2), to owe
decem, ten
***dein,** then
deinde, then
dēpōnō, -ōnere (3), **-osuī, -ositum,** to put down, set aside
***dēprōmō, -ōmere** (3), **-ōmpsī, -ōmptum,** to bring out, fetch
***dēsinō, -inere** (3), **-iī, -itum** (+ *infinitive*), to give up, stop
dēsistō, -istere (3), **-titī, -titum** (+ *infinitive*), to stop
deus, -ī (*m*), god
  ***dī,** nominative plural of **deus**
dīcō, -cere (3), **-xī, -ctum,** to say
  ***mala dīcere** (+ *dat.*), to curse, abuse
  ***male dīcere** (+ *dat.*), to curse, abuse
diēs, -ēī (*m*), day
difficilis, -is, -e, difficult
***dignus, -a, -um** (+ *abl.*), worthy
***dīligō, -igere** (3), **-ēxī, -ēctum,** to esteem, cherish, love
***disertus, -a, -um,** articulate, eloquent
***dispereō, -īre** (*irreg.*), **-iī, -itum,** to be ruined, perish, die
dissolvō, -vere (3), **-vī, -ūtum,** to dissolve, dispel, release
dīva, -ae (*f*), goddess
dīversus, -a, -um, diverse, different
***dīves, dīvitis,** wealthy, rich
***dīvus, -ī** (*m*), god
dō, dare (1), **dedī, datum,** to give
doleō (2), to grieve, be sorry, be pained
dolor, -ōris (*m*), grief, pain, anguish
domus, -ūs (*f*), house, home
dōnec, as long as
***dōnō** (1), to give as a gift, present
dormiō (4), to sleep
dūcō, -cere (3), **-xī, -ctum,** to lead, take
***dulcis, -is, -e,** sweet
dum, while, as long as

E

ē, ex (+ *abl.*), from, out of
effundō, -ndere (3), **-dī, -sum,** to pour forth, produce
ego, I
ēlegāns, -ntis, elegant, refined
enim (*postpositive*), for, in fact, because
eō, īre (*irreg.*), **iī, itum,** to go
ēripiō, -ipere (3), **-ipuī, -eptum,** to seize, take away
et, and
  et . . . et, both . . . and
etsī, although, even if
***excruciō** (1), to torture, torment
expellō, -ellere (3), **-pulī, -ulsum,** to drive out
exspectō (1), to await, look out for, anticipate

F

faciō, -ere (3), **fēcī, factum,** to make, produce
  iter facere, to travel
fallō, -ere (3), **fefellī, falsum,** to deceive, mislead
ferō, -rre (*irreg.*), **tulī, lātum,** to carry, bring, bear
fidēs, -eī (*f*), faith, trust
fīlia, -ae (*f*), daughter
fīnis, -is (*m*), end, (pl.) territory, land
fīō, fierī (*irreg.*), **factus sum,** to become, happen, take place
flamma, -ae (*f*), flame, fire
***flāvus, -a, -um,** yellow, golden-yellow
fleō, -ēre (2), **flēvī, flētum,** to cry over, weep over
***flōs, -ōris** (*m*), flower, blossom, bloom
***flūctus, -ūs** (*m*), wave
flūmen, -inis (*n*), river, stream
***foedus, -eris** (*n*), contract, pact, agreement
***fōns, fontis** (*m*), fountain, spring
***fōrmōsus, -a, -um,** beautiful, gorgeous
fortis, -is, -e, brave, strong
fortūna, -ae (*f*), fortune
frangō, -ere (3), **frēgī, frāctum,** to break, crush
frāter, frātris (*m*), brother
frāternus, -a, -um, brotherly
***frīgus, -oris** (*n*), cold, coldness
frūstrā, in vain, for nothing
fuga, -ae (*f*), flight
***fugāx, fugācis,** fleeing
fugiō, -ere (3), **fūgī,** to flee
***fulgeō, -gēre** (2), **-sī,** to shine, glitter

G

***gaudeō, -dēre** (2), **gāvīsus sum,** to rejoice, find delight, take pleasure
gēns, gentis (*f*), race, clan, (pl.) nations, peoples

genus, -eris (*n*), stock, descent, noble birth, lineage, offspring
***gradus, -ūs** (*m*), step, approach
***grāmen, -inis** (*n*), grass
grātiae, -ārum (*f pl*), thanks
    grātiās agere, to give thanks
grātus, -a, -um (+ *dat.*), pleasing
gravis, -is, -e, heavy, serious
***grex, gregis** (*m*), flock

H

habeō (2), to have, hold, consider
***Hadria, -ae** (*m*), the Adriatic Sea
Helena, -ae (*f*), Helen of Troy
***hērēs, -ēdis** (*m/f*), heir
hic, haec, hoc, this
hiems, -is (*f*), winter
homō, -inis (*m*), man, fellow
hōra, -ae (*f*), hour
horribilis, -is, -e, horrible, dreadful, terrible
hūc, to this place, to here, here
hūmānus, -a, -um, human

I

iam, now, already
    ***nōn iam**, no longer
ibi, there, then
īdem, eadem, idem, the same
ignis, -is (*m*), fire
ille, illa, illud, that, he, she, it
impōnō, -ōnere (3), **-osuī, -ositum** (+ *dat.*), to place on
in (+ *abl.*), in, on, among
in (+ *acc.*), into, onto
incolumis, -is, -e, safe, unharmed
***īnfacētus, -a, -um**, witless, dull-witted, crude
***īnfāmis, -is, -e**, ill-famed, notorious
***īnferiae, -ārum** (*f pl*), offerings for the dead, funeral rites
īnferō, -rre (*irreg.*), **intulī, illātum**, to bring in, introduce
***ingrātus, -a, -um**, unappreciated, thankless
iniūria, -ae (*f*), injury, wrongdoing
innumerābilis, -is, -e, innumerable, countless
inquam, I say
inquis, you say
īnsidiae, -ārum (*f pl*), ambush
inter (+ *acc.*), between, among
***invītus, -a, -um**, unwilling
iocus, -ī (*m*), joke
ipse, ipsa, ipsum, -self
īrātus, -a, -um, angry, agitated
is, ea, id, he, she, it
iste, ista, istud, this, that
ita, so, thus
Italia, -ae (*f*), Italy
Italus, -a, -um, Italian
iter, itineris (*n*), journey
    iter facere, to travel
iūcundus, -a, -um, delightful, pleasant

Iuppiter, Iovis (*m*), Jupiter

L

labor, labōris (*m*), work, labor
labōrō (1), to work, labor, suffer, struggle
***laetitia, -ae** (*f*), gladness, joy, delight
laetus, -a, -um, happy, joyous
***lateō** (2), to be concealed, hide
lātus, -a, -um, wide
legō, -ere (3), **lēgī, lēctum**, to read
***leō, leōnis** (*m*), lion
lēvis, -is, -e, light
līber, -era, -erum, free, freeborn
līberō (1), to free
licet, -ēre (2), **-uit** (+ *dat.* + *infinitive*), it is allowed, permitted
***lingua, -ae** (*f*), tongue, language
***linteum, -ī** (*n*), napkin
locus, -ī (*m; n in pl*), place
longus, -a, -um, long
loquor, -ī (3), **locūtus sum**, to speak, talk
lūx, lūcis (*f*), light
***lympha, -ae** (*f*), water

M

magis (*adv.*), rather, more
magnus, -a, -um, large, great, grand
maior, -ōris, greater
mālō, mālle (*irreg.*), **māluī** (+ *infinitive*), to prefer
malus, -a, -um, bad, evil
    ***mala dīcere** (+ *dat.*), to curse, abuse
    ***male dīcere** (+ *dat.*), to curse, abuse
maneō, -ēre (2), **-sī, -sum**, to remain, stay
manus, -ūs (*f*), hand
mare, -is (*n*), sea
māter, -tris (*f*), mother
māternus, -a, -um, maternal, on the mother's side
maximus, -a, -um, very great, greatest
mēns, -ntis (*f*), mind
***merum, -ī** (*n*), undiluted wine, wine
metuō, -ere (3), **-ī**, to fear
metus, -ūs (*m*), fear
meus, -a, -um, my
***mī**, dative of **ego**
mīlle, a thousand
    mīlia (*pl*), thousand, thousands
minimus, -a, -um, very small, smallest
minus (*adv.*), less
***mīrificus, -a, -um**, wonderful, marvelous
mīror, -ārī (1), **-ātus sum**, to wonder at, marvel at
miser, -era, -erum, miserable, wretched
mittō, -ere (3), **mīsī, missum**, to send
modo, recently
moneō (2), to warn
***mōnstrum, -ī** (*n*), wonder, portent, omen, monstrous creature
monumentum, -ī (*n*), monument, memorial
mora, -ae (*f*), delay

morior, -ī (3), **-tuus sum**, to die
moror, -ārī (1), **-ātus sum**, to delay, remain, dwell
mors, -tis (f), death
mortālis, -is (m), a mortal
mōs, mōris (m), custom
moveō, -ēre (2), **mōvī, mōtum**, to move, affect
mox, soon
mulier, -eris (f), woman
multus, -a, -um, much, great, considerable
  multī, -ae, -a, many
  multō (+ *comparative*), by much, much (more)
  multum (*adv.*), much
*****mūnus, -eris** (n), gift, offering
mūtō (1), to change
*****mūtus, -a, -um**, mute, silent
*****myrtus, -ī** (f), myrtle

N

nam, for
nārrō (1), to say, report
*****nāsus, -ī** (m), nose
nāvis, -is (f), ship
nāvita, -ae (m), sailor
nē (+ *subjunctive*), so that . . . not, lest
nec, neither, nor, and . . . not
  nec . . . nec, neither . . . nor
necesse, necessary
*****nefās** (n, *indeclinable*), violation, crime, wrongdoing
negō (1), to deny
nēmō, no one
neque, neither, nor
  neque . . . neque, neither . . . nor
nesciō (4), not to know
niger, -gra, -grum, black
nihil, nothing
nīl, nothing, not
*****nimium**, exceedingly, very
nisi, unless, if . . . not
*****niteō** (2), to shine, glitter
*****nix, nivis** (f), snow
nōbilis, -is, -e, noble, famous
noceō (2) (+ *dat.*), to harm, injure
nōlō, -lle (*irreg.*), **-luī**, to be unwilling, not wish
nōmen, -inis (n), name
nōn, not
  *****nōn iam**, no longer
  nōn sōlum, not only
nōnne, (introduces a question that expects the answer "yes")
nōs, we, us
nōscō, -scere (3), **-vī, -tum**, to come to know, (perfect) know, be acquainted with
noster, -tra, -trum, our
novus, -a, -um, new
nox, -ctis (f), night
nūllus, -a, -um, no, none
nūllus, -īus (m), no one, nobody

numerus, -ī (m), number, calculation
nunc, now
nūntius, -ī (m), messenger, message
Nympha, -ae (f), nymph

O

*****obdūrō** (1), to be firm, persist
*****occidō, -idere** (3), **-idī, -āsum**, to fall, set
Ōceanus, -ī (m), ocean
oculus, -ī (m), eye
omnis, -is, -e, all, every, each
onus, -eris (n), load, burden
oppōnō, -ōnere (3), **-osuī, -ositum**, to oppose
ops, -is (f), aid, assistance, help
optimus, -a, -um, best, very good, excellent
ōra, -ae (f), shore, coast
*****ōtium, -ī** (n), leisure, freedom from responsibility, idleness

P

pār, paris (+ *dat.*), equal
parēns, -ntis (m/f), parent, ancestor
parō (1), to prepare, furnish, acquire, obtain
pars, -tis (f), part, side
pater, -tris (m), father
*****patior, -tī, -ssus sum**, to permit, allow
paucī, -ae, -a, few
pavimentum, -ī (n), pavement, paved floor
per (+ *acc.*), through
*****perdō, -ere** (3), **-idī, -itum**, to destroy, ruin, lose
pereō, -īre (*irreg.*), **-iī, -itum**, to perish
*****perpetuus, -a, -um**, everlasting, continuous, uninterrupted
pēs, pedis (m), foot
pessimus, -a, -um, worst
petō, -ere (3), **-īvī, -ītum**, to seek, pursue
*****pietās, -ātis** (f), dutifulness, devotion
*****pius, -a, -um**, dutiful, grateful
placeō (2) (+ *dat.*), to please, appease
plūrēs, -ēs, -a, more
plūrimī, -ae, -a, most, very many
*****poēma, -atis** (n), poem
poēta, -ae (m), poet
pōnō, pōnere (3), **posuī, positum**, to place, put, put down, calm
*****pontifex, -icis** (m), priest
populus, -ī (m), people
portus, -ūs (m), port, harbor
possum, posse (*irreg.*), **potuī** (+ *infinitive*), to be able, can
postquam, after
potēns, -ntis, powerful, influential, ruling over (+ *gen.*)
*****potis, -is, -e**, possible
praeter (+ *acc.*), except
premō, -mere (3), **-ssī, -ssum**, to press
prīmus, -a, -um, first
prīnceps, -cipis, first, foremost, principal
prior, -ōris, former, earlier
prō (+ *abl.*), in return for, for
proelium, -ī (n), battle

proficīscor, -icīscī (3), **-ectus sum**, to set out, depart
prōvincia, -ae (f), province
puella, -ae (f), girl
puer, -erī (m), boy, young man, servant
pulcher, -chra, -chrum, beautiful
pūriter, purely, correctly, cleanly
putō (1), to think

Q

*__quā__, where
quaerō, -rere (3), **-sīvī, -sītum**, to look for, seek, ask, demand
quam, than, over
quantum, as, as much as
*__quārē__, for which reason, therefore
-que, and
quī, quae, quod, who, which, that
Quī . . . ? Quae . . . ? Quod . . . ?, What . . . ? Which . . . ?
quia, because
quīcumque, quaecumque, quodcumque, whoever, whatever
*__quis, quid__ (*after* **sī**), anybody, anything, somebody, something
Quis . . . ? Quid . . . ?, Who . . . ? What . . . ?
quisquam, quaequam, quicquam, anybody, anyone, anything
quisque, quaeque, quidque, each one
*__quō__ (*adv.*), to which place, to where
quod, because
*__quondam__, once
quoque, also, too
*__quot__, as many, however many

R

rapidus, -a, -um, quick, swift
rapiō, -ere (3), **-uī, -tum**, to snatch, seize
*__ratis, -is__ (f), boat, craft
recurrō, -rere (3), **-rī, -sum**, to run back, hurry back
reddō, -ere (3), **-idī, -itum**, to give back, return, render, grant
redeō, -īre (*irreg.*), **-iī, -itum**, to come back, return
redūcō, -cere (3), **-xī, -ctum**, to lead back
referō, -ferre (*irreg.*), **-ttulī, -lātum**, to bring back
rēgīna, -ae (f), queen
remittō, -ittere (3), **-īsī, -issum**, to send back, return
remōtus, -a, -um, remote, distant
renovō (1), to renew, revive, restore
reperiō, -perīre (4), **-pperī, -pertum**, to find
repetō, -ere (3), **-īvī, -ītum**, to seek again
reportō (1), to carry back
rēs, reī (f), thing, matter, affair, deed, circumstance
rēx, rēgis (m), king

rīdeō, -dēre (2), **-sī, -sum**, to laugh, laugh at
*__rīvus, -ī__ (m), stream
rogō (1), to ask for, beg
rosa, -ae (f), rose
ruīna, -ae (f), ruin, overthrow, destruction

S

sacer, sacra, sacrum, sacred
sagitta, -ae (f), arrow
*__sāl, salis__ (m), salt, humor, wit
salūs, -ūtis (f), health, salvation, means to recovery
Salvē! Salvēte!, Hello! Greetings!
*__sānctus, -a, -um__, sacred, holy, hallowed
saxum -ī (n), rock
*__scelus, -eris__ (n), crime
*__scīlicet__, certainly, clearly
sciō (4), to know
scrībō, -bere (3), **-psī, -ptum**, to write
sē, himself, herself, oneself, itself, themselves
secundus, -a, -um, second, next
sed, but
sedeō, -ēre (2), **sēdī, sessum**, to sit
semper, always
senex, senis (m), old man
sentiō, -tīre (4), **-sī, -sum**, to feel
sequor, -quī (3), **-cūtus sum**, to follow
serēnus, -a, -um, serene, calm
serpēns, -ntis (m/f), serpent, snake
servō (1), to save, preserve, protect, guard
seu, or if, or
  seu . . . seu, whether . . . or
sī, if
  sī quis, qua, quid, if anyone, if anything
sīc, thus, so
silva, -ae (f), forest, woods
similis, -is, -e (+ *dat.*), similiar to, like
simul, at the same time, together
  *__simul ac__, as soon as
*__sincērē__, sincerely, genuinely
sine (+ *abl.*), without
sinister, -tra, -trum, left
sīve . . . sīve, whether . . . or
sōl, -is (m), sun
sōlus, -a, -um, alone, only
  nōn sōlum, not only
soror, -ōris (f), sister
spectō (1), to look at
spērō (1), to hope, expect
spēs, -eī (f), hope, expectation
*__splendidus, -a, -um__, splendid, brilliant
stō, stāre (1), **stetī, statum**, to stand
suāvis, -is, -e, sweet, agreeable
sub (+ *abl.*), under, beneath
subdūcō, -cere (3), **-xī, -ctum**, to remove
subitō, suddenly
sum, esse (*irreg.*), **fuī, futūrus**, to be
sūmō, -mere (3), **-mpsī, -mptum**, to take up, put on
*__superbus, -a, -um__, magnificent, proud,

haughty
superō (1), to overcome, surpass
sustineō, -inēre (2), **-inuī, -entum**, to sustain, support, hold up
Syria, -ae (*f*), Syria

T

***taceō** (2), to be quiet
***tālis, -is, -e**, such, of this kind
tam, so, so much
tamen, nevertheless, however, still
tandem, finally, at last
tangō, -ere (3), **tetigī, tāctum**, to touch
tardus, -a, -um, slow
***taurus, -ī** (*m*), bull
tēcum, with you
***tellūs, -ūris** (*f*), land, ground
temptō (1), to try
tempus, -oris (*n*), time
teneō, -ēre (2), **-uī, -tum**, to hold
tergum, -ī (*n*), back
terra, -ae (*f*), land
timeō (2), to fear
timidus, -a, -um, frightened, fearful
timor, -ōris (*m*), fear
tollō, -ere (3), **sustulī, sublātum**, to lift up, steal
totidem, just the same
tōtus, -a, -um, entire, all, in every respect
trādō, -ere (3), **-idī, -itum**, to hand down
trēs, trēs, tria, three
***trīstis, -is, -e**, sad, dismal, gloomy
tū, you
   tēcum, with you
tum, then
tuus, -a, -um, your (singular)

U

ubi, where, when
ūllus, -a, -um, any
***umbra, -ae** (*f*), shade, shadow
umquam, ever
unde, from where, from which place

ūnus, -a, -um, one, single, only, merely
***urbānus, -a, -um**, urbane, sophisticated
urbs, -bis (*f*), city
***ūrō, -rere** (3), **-ssī, -stum**, to burn, (passive) be on fire
ut (+ *subjunctive*), in order to, so that, to
***ut**, as, how
ūtor, ūtī (3), **ūsus sum** (+ *abl.*), to use
uxor, -ōris (*f*), wife

V

Valē! Valēte! Good-bye!
valeō (2) (+ *infinitive*), to be strong, be able
vehō, -here (3), **-xī, -ctum**, to carry
vel, even, or
ventus, -ī (*m*), wind
Venus, -eris (*f*), Venus, goddess of love
***venustus, -a, -um**, charming, attractive, handsome
***vēr, vēris** (*n*), spring
verbum, -ī (*n*), word
vērē, truly, really
versus, -ūs (*m*), verse of poetry
***vērum**, but
vērus, -a, -um, true, real
vetus, -eris, old
via, -ae (*f*), road, way
videō, vidēre (2), **vīdī, vīsum**, to see
videor, vidērī (2), **vīsus sum**, to seem, appear
vīlla, -ae (*f*), farmhouse, country house
vīnum, -ī (*n*), wine
vir, virī (*m*), man, husband
virgō, -inis (*f*), maiden, vestal virgin
vīta, -ae (*f*), life
   vītam agere, to lead one's life
vītō (1), to avoid
vīvō, -ere (3), **vīxī, vīctum**, to live, be alive
vix, scarcely
vocō (1), to call
volō, velle (*irreg.*), **voluī**, to wish, be willing
   ***bene velle** (+ *dat.*), to be fond of, like, respect
volō (1), to fly
vulgus, -ī (*n*), crowd, masses

TEXT CREDITS AND SOURCES

Page 9: From *Catullus in English Poetry* by Eleanor Shipley Duckett, © 1972 by Russell & Russell, NY. Page 15: From *My Confidant, Catullus,* reprinted by Ives Street Press, © 1983 by Thomas McAfee. Page 19: Reprinted by permission of Faber and Faber Ltd from *The Translations of Ezra Pound,* © 1954 by Ezra Pound. Page 21: From *Literature of the Western World* (Vol. 1), "Chaucer's Canterbury Tales," translated by Theodore Morrison, © 1984 by Macmillan Publishing Co. From *The Complete Poems and Plays 1909–1950* by T.S. Eliot; Harcourt, Brace & World, Inc., NY, © 1971 by Esme Valerie Eliot. Page 23: From *Catullus in English Poetry* by Eleanor Shipley Duckett, © 1972 by Russell & Russell, NY. Page 24: From *Catullus in English Poetry* by Eleanor Shipley Duckett, © 1972 by Russell & Russell, NY. Page 25: From *Sappho and Alcaeus* by Denys Page, © 1955 by Oxford University Press, Ltd. Page 37: From *Roman Lyric Poetry: Catullus and Horace,* selected, with commentary by A.G. McKay and D.M. Shepherd; St. Martin's Press, NY, © 1969, 1974 by A.G. McKay and D.M. Shepherd; poem reprinted by permission from *The Hudson Review,* Vol. V, No. 1 (Spring 1952). Copyright © 1952 by The Hudson Review, Inc. Page 39: Reprinted by permission of Faber and Faber Ltd from *The Translations of Ezra Pound,* © 1954 by Ezra Pound; reprinted by permission from *The Poems of Catullus,* translated by Peter Whigham (Penguin Classics, 1966), copyright © Peter Whigham, 1966, p. 197; from *The Poems of Catullus,* translated by Horace Gregory; W.W. Norton & Co., Inc., © 1956 by Horace Gregory; reproduced by permission from *Roman Culture: Weapons and the Man,* edited by Gary Wills; George Braziller, Inc., © 1966 by Gary Wills. Page 43: From *Catullus in English Poetry* by Eleanor Shipley Duckett, © 1972 by Russell & Russell, NY. Page 47: Reproduced by permission from *The Hudson Review,* Vol. V, No. 1 (Spring 1952). Copyright © 1952 by The Hudson Review, Inc. Page 54: From *Ad Pyrrham, A Polyglot Collection of Translations,* edited by Ronald Starr, © 1955 by Oxford University Press. Page 63: From *Walt Whitman: The Complete Poems,* edited by Francis Murphy, © 1975 by Penguin Books Ltd. Page 71: From *Vergil: The Aeneid,* translated by W.F. Jackson Knight; Penguin Books Ltd., © 1956 by the Estate of G.R. Wilson Knight. Page 79: Reprinted by permission of the publishers and the Loeb Classical Library from *Lucretius: De Rerum Natura,* translated by W.H.D. Rouse and M.F. Smith, Cambridge, Mass.: Harvard University Press, Copyright © 1975. "Death Don't Have No Mercy" by Reverend Gary Davis, © 1968, Chandos Music (ASCAP).

PHOTOS

Page 7: SCALA/Art Resource, NY. Page 14: Lauros-Giraudon/Art Resource, NY. Page 22: Alinari/Art Resource, NY. Page 28: Marburg/Art Resource, NY. Page 34: The Bettmann Archive. Page 36: Reprinted from *Costumes of the Greeks and Romans* by Thomas Hope, © 1962 by Dover Publications, Inc., NY. Page 38: Alinari/Art Resource, NY. Page 40: Alinari/Art Resource, NY. Page 46: Reprinted from *Masterpieces of Greek and Roman Painting* by Ernst Pfuhl, translated by J.D. Beazley, © 1955 by Macmillan Publishing Co. Page 51: Reprinted from *Technology in the Ancient World* by Henry Hodges (drawings by Judith Newcomer); Alfred A. Knopf, Inc., © 1970 by Henry Hodges. Page 70: The Granger Collection, NY. Page 78: The Bettmann Archive. Page 83: The Bettmann Archive.